Collected Poems

Collected Poems

Flora Garry

GORDON WRIGHT PUBLISHING
25 MAYFIELD ROAD, EDINBURGH EH9 2NQ
SCOTLAND

British Library Cataloguing in Publication Data
A Catalogue for this book is available
from the British Library.

ISBN 0 903065 82 7

The publisher acknowledges subsidy from the
Scottish Arts Council towards the publication
of this volume.

The publisher acknowledges an award from the
Deric Bolton Poetry Trust towards the publication
of this volume.

The Publisher acknowledges an award from the
Charles Murray Memorial Fund towards
the publication of this volume.

Cover design: John Haxby.
Back cover photo: Gordon Wright.

Typeset by Gordon Wright Publishing Ltd., Edinburgh.
Printed and Bound by Butler & Tanner Ltd., Frome, Somerset.

Contents

This book is for the folk of New Deer village
and all who live by the Ugie and the Ythan in the
'braid Buchan lan' of North East Aberdeenshire.
This was our dialect and way of life.
This was our country.

Introduction

I am going to try to answer a few questions that have been put to me from time to time. First of all, why do I write? To answer that let me quote a remark of the late Benjamin Skinner, Headmaster of Strichen School. He knew the pedigrees of all his pupils and he would say, 'You may conjure the Devil out of your soul, but never your grandmother from your bones.'

Both my father and mother were writers: Archie Campbell, Buchan farmer, with his weekly article in the *Press and Journal* and Helen Campbell with her broadcast plays and beautiful voice. Our home out yonder at Auchmunziel was a place where people came for good music and lively talk, most of it in the Buchan dialect. Words. They were to us the breath of life.

My father even made them up. One was 'Jeelywabblichers'. He had been asked out for a genteel afternoon tea. That evening, back home, he said he was hungry and could do with some cheese and breid. Said my mother, 'Did ye nae get a good tea at Mrs So-and-So's?' 'Tea,' was his reply, 'Caa yon a tea? Naething worth ettin. Jist a puckle jeelywabblichers.' Ever after, that was our family name for fancy pieces, shivering jimmies and such like.

So, heredity comes into this writing business. To quote George Bruce:

> 'This which I write now
> Was written years ago
> Before my birth
> In the features of my father.'

My upbringing on a Buchan farm put a whole world at my disposal, a wealth of early impressions. Then came New Deer School, Peterhead Academy and four years at King's. I learned to recognise good writing and the importance of technique. But I didn't write much original stuff till the Second World War. Why not? I suppose the answer is that, as happiness has no history, neither does happiness write poetry. It needed wartime itself, with its emotional stress and upheaval, the feeling of danger, the future all unknown, to provide the necessary stimulus. At that time too, I was a member of a poetry-reading group in Dundee. We studied among other things the early lyrics of Hugh MacDiarmid and they opened new horizons. Then came a request for an entry to an Aberdeen Sangshaw. I wrote 'Bennygoak'. That was the beginning.

'Why verse rather than prose,' I have been asked. This, I think, stems from something very primitive, a feeling for rhythm. I find words and phrases making rhythmic patterns in my mind.

Sometimes I am asked: 'Why write in dialect and not in English?' This is easy. Because Scots is my mither tongue, associated with all sorts of early cherished memories – of home, landscape, folk, work, weather, songs, stories. I remember once – I would be about four – I fell into the horses' trough. I was running back to the house, dripping wet, when old Grandpa Metcalfe came out from the kitchen and took me by the hand round the kitchen door.

'Hie, some o you weemen,' he shouted, 'Tak an tirr this littlan. She's tummelt in o the horse troch an she's drookit like a droont moose.'

How could anybody, hearing day in, day out, speech of that sort, with its wealth of similes and metaphors, its rich resonant vowels and consonants, its strong rhythms and cadences, ever forget it, ever be ashamed of it?

But alas! That is exactly what happened to far too many of us. For after we went to school we came up against English speech and social snobbery. The laird, the ministers, the teachers all spoke English of a sort, the laird's English being different from the teachers' English, which made confusion worse confounded. Anxious, genteel mothers, looking to their children's future, poor ladies, banished that nasty broad Scots from their firesides and dinner tables. Scots speech was for the lower orders. Growing up for any child anywhere is a difficult enough business, but we in Buchan had the added complication of the two languages and their many variants. I suspect that much psychological harm resulted from the bilingualism, this confusion of languages, and that our so-called Buchan dourness is rather a form of speech-shyness.

But Buchan dialect is dangerous material: you can cover up thin platitudes with a fine, fine appearance: I've been guilty many times, I know.

Another question I have been asked is: 'Why do you write about folk and ways of fifty years ago. So much has happened since and is happening. Why not write about oil rigs rather than corn rigs?'

I could give the easy answer and say that was the Buchan I knew. But there's more to it than that. A poem isn't a statement of fact, a piece of reporting. It is created, made as a painting is made. Imagination takes one kind of reality and transforms it into another kind. It so happened that for me the Buchan folk and their language, generation after generation, the ferm toons, the skies, the parks, the teuchats all fused together in my mind to become the exciting raw stuff of poetry. Why, I don't know.

Most of my verses started with a single word or phrase with a tune in it, which kept on bothering me. The poem 'Bennygoak' stems from a scrap of conversation heard long ago in my grandmother's kitchen. She was saying to a neighbour: 'The man's fadder hid to tak it in fae the hedder an the funn.' These few words lay at the back of my mind for forty years and then, when a poem had to be written, they came to life and began to work like yeast, generating their own power. Once you get a seminal phrase the rest is just hard work, shaping and building.

A last question. One friend said: 'There's some gweed aneuch writin in yer bookie, but there's affa little aboot love.'

Love wasn't much mentioned in Buchan ferm toons except in a humorous off-taking fashion. Have you noticed how few good love poems there are in the poetry of the North East, apart from the old ballads?

Of course we knew love, all kinds of love, but it was not for speaking and writing about. All I saw of sexual love was illegitimate bairns, tears and gossip.

Of romantic love as in Violet Jacob's 'Tam i the Kirk' or Burns' 'O a' the Airts' we have nothing, or affa little.

Naturally we had our youthful dreams, our imaginative and romantic fantasies. And I remember with a certain wry amusement, the conspiracy of silence which surrounded those four-letter words scrawled on the walls of the stable. The horsemen's own cornkisters were not always acceptable! But our village concerts were crowded. There, with piano, fiddle and melodeon, with solo and duet singing – Burns, Bonnie Charlie, sentimental Victorian ballads, music-hall ditties – we found emotional outlet, while still preserving a modicum of reticence, of anonymity. Fit like folk? We are what we are.

Acknowledgements

I thank all the friends who encouraged me, chief among them the late Dr Cuthbert Graham of the *Aberdeen Press & Journal*. But an older and very special friend was my grandfather, James Metcalfe (1832-1917), who farmed Auchmunziel, New Deer, as did his father before him and my own father, Archie Campbell, followed by my brother after him. Grandpa Metcalfe was part of our family and was for me, mentor and loving companion all my young days. To him I owe all the knowledge I have of the Buchan 'spik'. I acknowledge too the unfailing support of my late husband, Robert Campbell Garry, who himself had roots in Buchan. To Gordon Wright, Publisher, I express appreciation of a recent pleasant and helpful association.

Flora Garry
Comrie, 1995.

Flora Campbell (13) with her grandfather James Metcalfe (82) photographed at home in New Deer in 1913. (Photo: A Norrie)

Poems in the Buchan Dialect

Flora Campbell at the age of twenty-five started teaching English at Strichen Secondary School (1925). A pupil was heard to comment, 'Aat canna be a teacher. She's ower bonny.' (photo: unknown)

Bennygoak

(The Hill of the Cuckoo)

It wis jist a skelp o the muckle furth,
A sklyter o roch grun,
Fin Granfadder's fadder bruke it in
Fae the hedder an the funn.
Granfadder sklatit barn an byre,
Brocht water to the closs,
Pat fail-dykes ben the bare brae face
An a cairt road tull the moss.

Bit wir fadder sottert i the yaard
An skeppit amo bees
An keepit fancy dyeuks an doos
At warna muckle eese.
He bocht aal wizzent horse an kye
An scrimpit muck an seed;
Syne, clocherin wi a craichly hoast,
He dwine't awaa, an dee'd.

Midder's growein aal an deen,
Dyle't an smaa-bookit tee.
Bit stull, she's maister o her wark.
My wark, it maisters me.
Och, I'm tire't o plyterin oot an in
Amo hens an swine an kye,
Kirnin amo brookie pots
An yirnin croods an fye.

I look far ower by Ythanside
To Fyvie's laich, lythe laans,
To Auchterless an Bennachie
An the mist-blue Grampians.
Sair't o the hull o Bennygoak
An scunnert o the ferm,
Gin I bit daar't, gin I bit daar't,
I'd flit the comin term.

wallach [handwritten margin note]

It's ull to thole on the first Spring day
Fin the black earth lies in clods,
An the teuchat's wallochin to the ploo
An the snaa-bree rins on the roads.
O, it's ull to thole i the stull hairst gloam,
Fin the lift's a bleeze o fire;
I stan an glower, the pail i ma han,
On ma road oot tull the byre.

Bit it's warst avaa aboot Wutsunday
Fin the nichts are quaet an clear,
An the flooerin curran's by i the yaard
An the green corn's i the breer;
An the bird at gid this hull its name,
Yon bird ye nivver see,
Sits doon i the wid by the water-side
An laachs, laich-in, at me.

'Flit, flit, ye feel,' says the unco bird,
'There's finer, couthier folk
An kinlier country hine awaa
Fae the hull o Bennygoak.'
Bit ma midder's growein aal an deen
An likes her ain fireside.
Twid brak her hert to leave the hull:
It's brakkin mine to bide.

skelp: *sizeable area*. muckle furth: *great out-of-doors*. sklyter: *expanse*. roch grun: *rough ground*. hedder: *heather*. funn: *whin; gorse*. closs: *close*. fail-dykes: *low turf walls*. sottert: *pottered about*. skeppit: *handled bee-hives (skeps)*. dyeuks: *ducks*. doos: *pigeons*. eese: *use*. bocht: *bought*. aal: *old*. wizzent: *shrunken*. scrimpit: *stinted*. syne: *then*. clocherin: *coughing frequently*. craichly hoast: *catarrhal cough*. dwine't awaa: *physically deteriorated; faded away*. dyle't: *toilworn*. smaa-bookit: *shrunken*. plyterin: *squelching*. kirnin: *messing about*. brookie: *sooty*. yirnin: *curdling*. croods an fye: *curds and whey*. laich: *low*. lythe: *shelter*. sair't: *to have one's fill of*. scunnert: *fed up*. flit: *go away; clear out*. ull to thole: *hard to bear*. teuchat: *lapwing*. wallochin: *wailing*. snaa-bree: *slush*. hairst gloam: *harvest sunset*. lift's a bleeze: *sky's a blaze*. warst avaa: *worst of all*. quaet: *quiet*. breer: *brier*. gid: *gave*. laachs: *laughs*. laich-in: *quietly*. couthier: *homelier*. hine awaa: *far away*. bide: *remain*.

14

Spring Fever

The tinkers tire o cassey steens fin Mey dyow weets the leys.
They seek eence mair the Buchan road, the wide win-cairdit skies.
Throwe Cloverhill an Tarbothill, by Blairton's cottar raa,
The braes o Logie, Foveran's howe, the wids o Turnerha.
By Essyfaal an Tillymaal, the walks o Neddermeer
An the girssy double dykes at clim to the lang toon o New Deer.

Syne hey for Cyaak an Cyaarneywhing
Bracklamore an Bennymeen,
Scoor the boords o Leddysfoord
An skum the lums o Glesslaw.

The yalla blossom's on the funn, o livrock-sang there's rowth,
A bluffert aff the bare broon knowes brings a waff o burnin grouthe.
Bit the aal wife on the breist o the cairt, tit-tittin at the rynes,
She sees the siller saxpences o the gypit kitchie quines.
The young wife, cooryin i the strae, a littlin happit close,
Sees at even the peat reek rise an hears the pipes i the moss.

The tink sits sidelins on the float, a cowt atween the theats,
A skweengin bikk ahin the wheels an a smarrach o barfit geets.
His min's on besoms, caups an pins an sowderin fite-iron,
An mowdiewarts' an myaakins' skins, an troots i the Gonar burn.

So they'll nae devaal by Tarty's waal,
Nor daachle lang at Udny.
The hedder hulls afore them lie,
Their simmer hame Turlundie.

cassey steens: *causeway stones*. dyow: *dew*. leys: *grassy fields*. win-cairdit: *wind-driven*.
scoor: *scour*. boords: *boards*. skum: *skim*. funn: *whin; gorse*. livrock: *laverock*. rowth:
profusion. bluffert: *squall of wind*. knowes: *steep fields; braes*. waff: *faint scent*. grouthe:
weeds. gypit kitchie quines: *foolish kitchen girls*. cooryin: *cowering*. littlin: *child*. happit:
well wrapped. reek: *smoke*. tink: *gypsy*. sidelins: *sideways*. cowt: *colt*. theats: *traces*.
skweengin bikk: *scrounging bitch*. smarrach: *swarm*. barfit geets: *barefoot children*.
besoms: *brooms*. caups an pins: *wooden bowls and clothes pegs*. sowderin: *soldering*.
fite-iron: *tin-plate*. mowdiewarts: *moles*. myaakins: *hares*. devall: *halt*. waal: *well*.
daachle: *linger*.

15

The Professor's Wife

I wis a student at King's.
Ma folk hid a craft in Glenardle.
'Learnin's the thing,' they wid say,
'To help ye up in the wardle.'

They vrocht fae daylicht to dark.
Fine div I min' on ma midder,
Up ower the queets amo dubs,
Furth in the weetiest widder.

Swypin the greep in the byre,
Forkin the crap on the laan,
Treetlin wi water an aess an peats,
Aye a pail in her haan.

I wis a student at King's.
O the craft I nivver spoke.
Peer and prood wis I
An affrontit o ma folk.

An fyles on a stull Mey nicht
I wid tak a daaner roun
By Spital an College Bounds
To the lythe o the Aal Toon.

An I wid stan an glower
In at the windows wide
O the muckle hooses there
Far the professors bide.

At cannle-licht an flooers
Shinin silver an lace,
An, braw in a low-neckit goon,
The professor's wife at her place.

'Fine,' says I to masel,
'Fine to be up in the wardle,'

An thocht wi a groo, on the brookie pots
In the kitchen at Glenardle.

'Learnin's the thing,' says I,
'To help ye up in the wardle.'
I wed a professor come time
An gid hyne awaa fae Glenardle.

I bide in a muckle dark hoose
In a toon that's muckle an dark,
An it taks me maist o the day
To get fordalt wi ma wark.

Traachlin wi sitt an styoo.
Queuein for maet for oors,
A body his little time or hert
For cannle-licht an flooers.

Ma hans are scorie-hornt,
An fyles I fin masel
Skushlin ma feet, as ma midder did
Oot teemin the orra pail.

The aal folk's lyin quaet
In the kirkyard at Glenardle.
It's as weel; they'd be gey sair-made
At the state noo-a-days o the wardle.

'Learnin's the thing,' they wid say,
'To gie ye a hyste up in life.'
I wis eence a student at King's.
Noo I'm jist a professor's wife.

---

craft: *croft.* wardle: *world.* vrocht: *worked.* queets: *ankles.* greep: *gangway.* crap: *crop.*
treetlin: *trotting.* aess: *ashes.* affrontit: *embarrassed.* fyles: *sometimes.* daaner: *wander.*
lythe: *shelter.* glower: *glare.* groo: *shudder.* brookie: *sooty.* hyne awaa: *far away.* bide:
reside. fordalt: *well ahead.* traachlin: *struggling.* sitt an styoo: *soot and dust.* maet: *meat;
food.* scorie-hornt: *calloused.* skushlin: *shuffling.* teemin: *emptying.* orra pail: *slop pail.*
gey sair-made: *hard pressed.* hyste up: *help up.* eence: *once.*

The Cat

A free translation of 'Le Chat' from
Baudelaire's *Les Fleurs du Mal.*

Big, bonny cat-beast, douce an tame,
Ye wanner roun ma kitchen fleer
An wanner throwe ma thochts; I'll sweir
That there ye've fun a second hame.

Fyles ye myurr-myurr to me ma leen,
Yer quaverin myowies thin an smaa,
Sae saft they're scarce a soun avaa.
Ye're couthy in yer fraisin teen.

Bit fyles yer birss begins to rise
An rummlins fae yer thrapple birl
Wi fearsome gurr an feerious dirl
Like thunner rivin simmer skies.

Fin I'm owercome wi warldly care
An dwine in dark despondency,
Ye'll come, ma cat, an purr to me
Yer three-threids-an-a-thrum I'll hear.

An syne ma waesome wechty fraacht
Growes licht, yer sangie warms ma veins
Like some aal ballad's liltin strains
Or like a love-brew's heidy draacht.

I've hard fiddle tunes sae rare
An sweet they'd thowe a hert o steen
An fire the caalest bleed, bit neen
Wi yours, ma bawdrons, can compare.

Ye're a dumb breet, nae wirds hiv ye,
Yet aa the joys by Man e'er pree'd
Yer tongue can tell; na, ye've nae need
To spiel a lang langamachie.

18

Cam ye fae some idder warl,
Mysterious, oonchancy cat,
A speerit-craiter athoot faat,
To me, a feel, roch human carl?

This hoose is yours, the gear, the folk
Ootside an in, baith but an ben.
Aa wir concerns ye beet to ken.
Are ye a god or deevilock?

I min' ae nicht, fin straikin ye,
Yer coat o yalla tortyshell
Ceest on the air a balmy smell,
Its sweet reek yoamt aa ower me.

To watch ye is a richt divert,
Ma een as by a lodesteen draan.
Siccar ye grip me, an I'm thraan
To turn to my ain thochts, to pairt

Fae you. Bit stull an on I'll see,
In my min's benmost neuk, I'll sweir,
Like bleezin cwyles o caal green fire
Yer twaa een glowerin straacht at me.

N Known
to PC.

IL sing.

douce: *gentle; lovable*. fyles: sometimes. ma leen: *alone*. fraisin teen: *ingratiating mood*.
birss: *temper*. thrapple: *throat*. gurr: *growl*. feerious: *furious*. dirl: *rumble*. rivin: *tearing*.
dwine: *pine*. three-threids-an-a-thrum: *cat's purr*. waesome wechty fraacht: *sorrowful
weighty load*. draacht: *draught*. thowe: *thaw*. bawdrons: *pussycat*. breet: *brute*. pree'd:
tasted. spiel: *recite*. langamachie: *rigmarole*. oonchancy: *not safe to meddle with*. feel:
foolish. roch: *rough*. carl: *fellow; chap*. gear: *accoutrements*. beet to ken: *need to know*.
deevilock: *little devil*. straikin: *stroking*. ceest: *cast*. yoamt: *eddied*. richt divert:
entertainment. lodesteen: *magnet*. siccar: *sure*. thraan: *unwilling*. benmost neuk:
innermost part. cwyles: *glowing embers*.

19

Foo Aal's Bennachie?

'Foo aal's Bennachie? As aal's a man?'
Loon-like I wid speir, an leave ma bools
A boorach in the kypie at ma feet
An stan an stare oot ower the darknin laan
Ower parks an ferms, as far's ma een could see
To the muckle hull aneth the settin sun.
'Aaler, laddie, aye, gin Man himsel.
Naebody kens the age o Bennachie.'

The years gid in. The bools war putten by.
Like mony anidder Buchan loon sin syne,
Rivven atween the Deil an the Deep Sea,
I swiddert far to turn, fit road to try.
Hamewith, Deil o the ferm, wark's weird to dree,
The sizzons' quaet, slow-fittit tyranny?
Awaa, Deep Sea o learnin an strange folk,
The oonchancy wardle furth o Bennachie?

Bit aa this time the hull wis company,
Pairt o baith my wardles, lookin doon
Sae freenly-like at ploo an hairst an hyowe.
Though aften, tee, a shape o fantasy.
Ararat, the Banks o Italie,
Soracte far the drift lay oxter-deep,
Atlas, Athabasca, Helicon,
The mountains o the Moon war Bennachie.

Byeuks an learnin took me i the eyn.
Amid the big toons' fyaacht an dirdumdree
The Buchan parks an skies gid oot o min',
Ma dreams hid idder shapes gin Bennachie.
Ae simmer day, I climt yon knowe eence mair
An lookit far ootower ma ain country,
Ower dykes an steadins, trees an girss an corn
To the wast, to the Mither Tap o Bennachie.

Bit smilin there, she wis nae pairt o me.
I wis a stranger chiel in a strange laan,
An ootlin wannert back by some mischance
To tak a teet at the place far he eest to be.
Foo aal's Bennachie? As aal's a man?
Ageless, timeless she, the fickle jaad.
Lichtsome, hertless she, the bonny quine.
I've been ower lang awaa. It's me that's an aal man.

foo aal?: *how old?* loon-like: *boy-like.* speir: *enquire.* boorach: *cluster.* kypie: *hollow.* sin
syne: *since then.* swiddert: *swithered.* hamewith: *back home.* weird to dree: *destiny to
fulfil.* sizzons': *seasons'.* oonchancy: *dangerous.* wardle: *world.* hairst an hyowe: *harvest
and hoe.* byeuks: *books.* fyaacht: *stress.* dirdumdree: *routine.* ootlin: *alien.* tak a teet: *take
a peep.* jaad: *perverse woman.* quine: *young girl.*

Ae Mair Hairst

She promised weel aneuch – a heavy crap.
Bit a dull, mochy Simmer it wis, wi affa little drooth.
Some o's, ye'll min', gey forcey, cuttit ower green,
An syne the widder broke.

Caal, roch shooers drave doon on a nor-east win.
The cattle oot on the girss
Wannert wi their backs up roun the dykes,
Nivver ristin.
Aye the onding, aye the clorty dubs.
I' the howe o Ythan wik efter weary wik
The stooks steed tasht an water-loggit.
Mornin efter mornin yon fite haar
Cam blaain in fae the coast.

Bit ae foreneen the win swang roun to the wast,
The cloods were heich an licht,
The sky wis blue-er gin we'd seen't aa Simmer.
The howes firmt up. The strae began to reeshle.
Shaef efter shaef we turnt the stooks wi wir hans
In tull the face o a strong sunshiny breeze.
I' the cornyards, the smell o the ripent grain.

We workit hard, fyles by the licht o the meen,
Fyles on the Sabbath day,
An we got her aff the grun, ae mair hairst!
An noo fae Mormond Hill as far's Bennachie,
The raikit stibble parks lie teem an quaet,
Wytin for the ploo.

---

aneuch: *enough.* crap: *crop.* mochy: *muggy.* affa: *awful.* drooth: *drought.* gey forcey: *too eager.* widder: *weather.* caal, roch shooers: *cold, rough showers.* girss: *grass.* ristin: resting.* onding: *downpour.* clorty: *sticky.* howe: *hollow; valley.* tasht: *knocked about; dishevelled.* fite haar: *white frost.* reeshle: *rustle.* fyles: *sometimes.* ae mair hairst: *one more harvest.* teem an quaet: *empty and quiet.* wytin: *waiting.* ploo: *plough.*

The Quine an the Teuchats

Nicht's creepin in aboot, it's early lowsin-time.
Ahin the laich funn dyke, licht's hinmost lowe,
A smaa reid cwyle, smores i the reek o the rime.
An icy skimmerin lappers the troch mou.
The nyaakit bourtree's gapin for the snaa.
The day's deen. The year's at the deid-thraa.

On the ploo'd eynriggs o the stibble park
A flock o teuchats gedder, cooryin doon
Atween the furrs an chunnerin i the dark;
Tappit heids an chilpit chudderin breists
Seekin some strab o strae or twaa-three faal
O girss, to hap them fae the sypin caal.

Bit the Spring o the year'll thowe the nirlt grun,
Slocken the gizzent gowan-reet, kennle the funn,
An wallochy-wallochy-weet the teuchats rise
Ower the new-shaaven leys.

Faar syne will I flee
Fae floorish on tree,
Sin bricht i the lift,
Burn birlin i the licht?
Fit bield syne hap me,
Faa winter-sted maan be
Eyven at Simmer's hicht?

teuchat: *lapwing.* lowsin-time: *time to stop work.* laich: *low.* funn dyke: *whin dyke.*
hinmaist: *last.* lowe: *gleam.* cwyle: *glowing ember.* smores: *smothers; chokes.* reek:
smoke. rime: *frost.* lappers: *freezes; curdles.* troch: *trough.* nyaakit: *naked.* deid-thraa:
death-throe. gedder: *gather.* cooryin: *cowering.* chunnerin: *murmuring plaintively.* tappit
heids: *tufted heads.* chilpit: *chilled.* chudderin: *shivering.* twaa-three faal: *a few folds.*
girss: *grass.* hap: *cover.* sypin: *seeping.* thowe: *thaw.* nirlt: *shrivelled.* slocken: *slake.*
gizzent: *dried up.* gowan-reet: *daisy root.* kennle the funn: *kindle the whin.* leys: *fields.*
bield: *shelter.* winter-sted: *beset by winter.*

War: 1939-1945

'Faar's Baabie Jeanie's loon? The aal wife hersel
Stans treeshin hame the milkers at the ley park yett.
Faa caas the mornin cairt an fordals neeps an strae,
Wi waages up an risin an fee'd folk sae ull to get?
Baabie Jeanie's Jockie, faar's he?

An yon swack hashin chiel in Willum Sinclair's shop?
He heeld ye oot o langour, sae joco an kin'ly wi't.
'Noo, lassie' to the grunnies: 'Weel, dearie' to the quines,
He's a want ahin the coonter, Willum's sic a strunge breet.
I miss a news wi yon lad. Faar's he?

An Droggie's clivver dother? She could mak her fadder's peels.
Nae hoven wyme or clocher, nae beelin, hack or strain
Bit she could ease; an fin royt nackets tummelt greetin at their play
She'd rowe up their bleedit sair bits, sen them duncin furth again.
The bairns likit Chrissie. Faar's she?

An Cyaarnadellie's foreman? I' the clear Spring nichts
He trystit wi the banker's deemie up at the market place.
Noo, she's skycin roun the gable-eyn, her leen, i the early gloam,
Wi a muckle cwyte aboot her an a graavit ower her face.
Cyaarnadellie's foreman, faar's he?'

* * *

'Speir at the waarslin tides, the desert saans, the caal starlicht.
They ken far.'

treeshin: *calling; enticing.* yett: *gate.* fordals: *stores.* swack: *agile.* hashin: *hustling.*
heeld ye: *held you.* langour: *boredom.* joco: *jovial.* quines: *young girls.* strunge breet:
surley chap. droggie: *the chemist.* peels: *pills.* hoven wyme: *swollen stomach.* clocher:
cough. beelin: *festering sore.* royt nackets: *boisterous children.* trystit: *met regularly;*
'dated'. deemie: *maid; general servant.* skycin: *skurrying.* her leen: *alone.* cwyte: *coat.*
graavit: *scarf.* speir: *enquire.*

Spring on a Buchan Ferm

Ower lang we've tholed the sizzon's tyranny,
Winter's hivvy wecht on man an beast,
Ower lang the dark, the snaa, the sypin caal.

Noo, on a suddenty, the lift's rivven wide.
Hivvenly licht poors doon an blins an droons
The dozent, thowless wardle. Snaa-bree loups,
Ice-tangles fae the eezins dreep, the Furth
New quickent blinks an glinters i the sin.
A livrock oot o sicht amo smaa cloods
Sings as at Creation's mornin oor.
An yonner by the ivied gairden dyke
A vraithe o snaadraps, livrock-sang in flooer.

Syne, on the indraacht o a breath, the lift gloams ower.
Daylicht's deen an Winter's back again.
Reet, reef an steen, the glancin pirlin burn
Shacklt eence mair; nae heat, nae colour noo
In park or steadin or in corn yaard
Bit the yalla sharn midden's smuchterin fire
An a muckle vraithe o trampit bleedy snaa
Far late the streen we beeriet a deid hogg.

Doon comes pick mirk, an hunger, birth an pain
Ride upo the riggin o the nicht.
The lammin yowie yammers fae the bucht,
The rottan's pykit teeth chudder the barley seck,
The skweengin hoolet clooks the moosie's wyme,
The ravenous futtrit sooks the livrock's breist.

Treachery, a broken tryst, at's a Buchan Spring;
Glory, an syne hertbrak, a sair oonchancy thing.

tholed: *endured.* on a suddenty: *suddenly.* lift: *sky.* rivven: *pulled apart.* dozent: *half asleep.* thowless: *inert.* wardle: *world.* snaa-bree: *slush.* eezins: *eaves.* vraithe: *wreath.* indraacht: *drawing in; inhaling.* reet: *root.* reef: *roof.* pirlin: *rippling.* smuchterin: *smouldering.* the streen: *last night.* pick mirk: *pitch dark.* yammers: *cries out.* rottan: *rat.* hoolet: *owl.* clooks: *claws.* wyme: *stomach.* futtrit: *weasel.* oonchancy: *unpredictable.*

To Suffie, Last o the Buchan Fishwives

A fish creel wi a wife aneth't
Steed at wir kitchen door.
A smaa quine grat at the wild-like shape
She'd nivver seen afore.

Ye cam fae anidder warl, Suffie,
Amo hiz lanward folk,
The sough o the sea in the verra soun
O the wirds ye spoke.

Oor wyes warna yours, we nivver vrocht
Wi net nor line
Nor guttin knife, nor fan on haggert thoom
The stang o the brine.

We nivver hid to flee demintit
Tull the pier-heid,
Nor harken tull the heerican at midnicht,
Caal wi dreid.

Spring efter Spring, or the teuchat's storm wis past
Ye wannert the road,
Heid tull the sleety win an boo't twaa-faal,
Shoodrin yer load.

Simmer parks war kinlier tull yer feet
Gin steens an styoo.
Bit fyles the stirkies chased ye.
Faa wis feart? Them or you?

Yon bricht huddry buss that wis eence yer hair
Is grizzilt noo,
An ower lang scannin o the sea his bleacht
Yer een's blue.

Wark an dule an widder sharpit yer face
Tull skin ower been,
As the tides tormint an futtle
A smaa fite steen.

Weel, umman, noo it's lowsin-time, we wuss
For you a fylie's ease;
Syne, at the hinmost waa-gyaan,
Quaet seas.

aneth't: *beneath it.* smaa quine: *small girl.* anidder warl: *another world.* grat: *wept.*
sough: *sigh; murmur.* vrocht: *worked.* haggert thoom: *hacked thumb.* teuchat's storm: *a
cold snap in April with snow showers.* boo't twaa-faul: *bent two-fold; stooping.* shoodrin:
shouldering. steens an styoo: *stones and dust.* huddry buss: *wind-blown bush.* grizzilt:
turning grey. wark an dule: *labour and sorrow.* been: *bone.* futtle: *whittle.* umman:
woman. lowsin-time: *time to stop work; to unyoke.* wuss: *wish.* fylie's ease: *time of
peace.* hinmost: *last.* waa-gyaan: *going away; departure.*

27

Sweet Cicely

We caad it myrrh. It cam at the bare time
O lang blae licht an broon new-shaaven ley,
Skwylin teuchat, reek o burnin grouth,
The caal Gab o Mey.

Throwe June's lown days, ower craft an ferm toon
In flooerin froth its sounless green tide broke,
Happin trails o weer an clooert pails,
Roosty speens an smaa bleacht birdies' beens,
Wallydraigle Winter's orra troke.

Aa Simmer chucknies pickit in its shade,
Dyeuks laid awaa an cats their kittlins hade.
An quinies, biggin their lame hoosies, raxed
To pu the sappy, feddry leaves an snuff
Their wersh-sweet guff.

Cam clyack, rummlin cairts, the hairst meen.
Stilpert myrrh stalks bore their tines o seeds,
Stumps o shammelt teeth in aal men's heids.
Syne it wis dark or lowsin-time.
The myrrh wis geen.

Bit ae black, bitter nicht i the year's deid thraa –
Nicht o Redemption, the Nativity –
A waakrife littlin raise an, teetin furth,
Saw aneth a nyaakit elder tree,
Lowein i the licht o nae earthly Spring,
The myrrh fite-flooerin for a Bairn King.

blae: *a cold blue colour.* ley: *field.* Gab o Mey: *early in May.* lown: *mild.* weer: *wire.*
clooert: *battered.* speens: *spoons.* beens: *bones.* wallydraigle: *draggletail.* orra troke:
debris. chucknies: *young chickens.* dyeuks: *ducks.* kittlins: *kittens.* quinies: *small girls.*
biggin: *building.* lames: *fragments of broken crockery collected by little girls to play
with.* raxed: *stretched.* wersh-sweet guff: *slightly unpleasant smell.* clyack: *when the corn
is all cut but not stacked.* hairst meen: *harvest moon.* stilpert: *spindly.* tines: *spikes.*
shammelt: *uneven.* lowsin-time: *time to stop work.* geen: *gone.* deid thraa: *death throe.*
waakrife: *wakeful.* teetin furth: *peeping out.* nyaakit: *naked.* lowein: *glowing.*

Snow and Sea

(An aal fisherman looks at Joan Eardley's painting)

Caa yon wir shore-road? Mair like sitt-black coo-branks
Haadin agen yon loupin beast the sea.
Caa yon snaa-vraithes? Runkelt yalla hippens
Happin the bents an the lanward ferm country.
Yon a shooer? Feerious birlin sleet-raips
Twinet b' the heerican's thraa-heuks i the lift.
An faar's wir fisher toon? Ae lum, ae gaivel
Blinterin throwe blae watter an smore drift.

I kent aa richt. Ower weel. Nae picter nott.
On sic a nicht the *Nellie Gatt* gid doon
Twaa mile aff Dunnottar an took wi 'er
Sin an bridder an a sister's loon.
Anidder nicht – Na! Na! I'd nivver daar
Gie yon hoose-room.

I steed the dirl, umman, lang or ye vrocht pent.
Shoodert ma birn o dool or ye kent meen fae starns.
As weel frame a swatch o ma ain harns,
Set hert's bleed on ma mantel-piece for ornament.

Awaa! Aal folk like me
Fain wid be latten be,
Wir waarslin ower.
I'll sit i the lythe door, the blue air,
Thocht's tide slack, at ease,
Simmer's kin'ly han upo ma knees.
Upo ma waa a calendar or twaa,
A joog o jassamine,
A kittlin clookin at a cloo,
A littlin, laachin.

coo-branks: *cattle shackles.* snaa-vraithes: *snow-wreaths.* hippens: *diapers.* feerious: *furious.* sleet-raips: *ropes of sleet.* thraa-heuks: *twisting hooks.* lift: *sky.* gaivel: *gable.* blae watter: *grey-blue water.* smore drift: *smothering snow.* nott: *required.* steed the dirl: *coped with my responsibilities.* umman: *woman.* vrocht pent: *practised your art.* birn o dool: *burden of sorrow.* harns: *brains.* lythe: *shelter.* clookin: *clawing.* cloo: *ball of wool.*

Village Magdalen

Yon wis nivvir a wird to lichtlify.
'Hooer o Babylon', bleed-jeelin, Bible
Wird o pooer, stern, magic, tribal.
Deleeriet drunks wid lift it, fechtin mad,
Or haflins swicket b' some mim-moo'd jaad
An hotterin i their ain young hell;
Bit nae afore a bairn, nor tull a beast,
An nae tull Bell.

She bade in a bothy doon Steenybrae Lane.
She'd a yaard an a stackie o peats,
A rain-water bowie, a lang hippen-towie,
An aye the aal coach an the smarrach o geets.

Hushelt intull a man's cassen waterproof cwyte
An a pair o hol't tackety beets,
An humfin a pyockfu o tatties or meal,
Or a birn o rozetty reets.

Skushlin ben the dutch-side, her milk flagon in han,
Dyl't-lookin an worth i the queets,
Michty, faa'd lie ben the bowster fae yon,
An faa the earth faddert yon geets?

She wisna aa come, said some. At's as may be.
She wis washin ae day at Burngrain
Wi yon muckle maasie on. Burnie's wife scraichs:
'Lordsake, Bella, nae surely again?'

An says Bell, wi a dour kin o thraa tull her moo,
Aa the time timmerin on wi the sheets:
'We canna jook fit lies afore's. It's jist Fate
At's geen me aa yon smarrach o geets.'

Pooerfu, barritchfu wirds hae thir time an place.
Bit less preceesion fyles may meet the case
An dee less ull.

30

Better a kin'ly gley gin a dirten glower.
Easier to cower.
Sae caa her sleekit, saft, a throwder baggerel.
Bit hooer? Na, nae Bell.

lichtlify: *treat lightly.* bleed-jeelin: *blood-curdling.* deleeriet: *demented.* haflins: *youths.*
swicket: *cheated.* mim-moo'd jaad: *tight-lipped, prudish, perverse woman.* hotterin:
seething. hippen-towie: *clothes rope for drying diapers outdoors.* coach: *pram.* smarrach
o geets: *swarm of brats.* hushelt: *huddled.* cassen: *faded.* cwyte: *coat.* beets: *boots.*
humfin: *carrying laboriously.* pyockfu: *bagful.* birn o rozetty reets: *heavy burden of
resinous logs.* dyl't-lookin: *toilworn.* worth i the queets: *crippled around the ankles.*
bowster: *bolster.* faddert: *fathered.* aa come: *all there, sane.* maasie: *jersey.* scraichs:
screeches. thraa: *twist.* timmerin on: *working vigorously.* jook: *avoid; dodge.* barritchfu:
harsh. gley: *squint.* dirten glower: *contemptuous stare.* cower: *recover from.* throwder
baggerel: *slovenly, shapeless female.*

Flora with her husband Professor Robert Campbell Garry at their home, Laich Dyke,
Comrie, 15 August 1979. (Photo: *The Scots Magazine*).

Figures Receding

There's twaa wyes o kennin —
Wi yer heid, yer rizzon an muckle respec
For the weel-stored min';
Wi yer finger-eyns, yer instincts an yer een,
Lear o anidder kin'.

Charlie traivelt a staig.
They rampag't up the closs in cloods o styoo.
The smaa steens skytit aff the barn sklates.
Dogs bowfft, hens kecklt an flew.
Meers nichert i the clover park, took roun the dykes,
The bairns war dreelt to the hoose.
The kitchie lass tichent her steys.
The gweed wife lat doon her broos.
A smaa, reid-mowsert chiel, I min', wi a mad look in his ee,
Far ben i the Horseman's Wird.
Fin suppert he'd roar an sing,
The melodeon on his knee,
'The Dowie Dens', 'Drumdelgie', 'Lang John More',
Syne mak for the deemie's sleepin place wi'ts open door.

Bit early ae day, efter Aikey Fair,
He wis gotten nyaakit ower by Mains o Glack,
Face doon in a dutch, a gully knife in's back.

Kirsty cairriet a pack an bade in a lair i the moss.
A toozy, sinbrunt wife in a tartan shawl,
Reengin the roads wi geets an a tyke at her heel,
Gabbin laich-in tull hersel an wadgin her nieve
At her ain face glowerin up throwe Strypie's waal.
She swallit puddock steels,
Turnt horse hair intull eels,
Kent fit made yon oorlich skraichin souns
An the bobbin greenichty lichts
I' the moss on winter nichts.
An eence she saw the Deil
Skookin ahin a waggin black breem buss.

32

She deet atween fite sheets, in her ninetieth year
In a dother's cooncil hoose aside Aal Deer.

Johnnie muckit the byre – a big, fite-winkert man,
Slow, bashfu amo folk,
Bit see him calve a coo or drog a stirk
Or set a dreepin stook tull een o'clock.
He nott nae byeuks to read
The meer's tail cloods,
A nieve-fu o new-thrasht corn,
Fitt rot in a hirplin yowe,
Neeps ready for the hyowe;
Widder an beasts an lan,
The wark that lay tull his han.

They say he's aye to the fore,
Some blin an crulgie doon,
Gey dottelt fyles, bit chief wi aa the bairns,
An aye on the meenit heid, fin pension day comes roun.

There's twaa wyes o kennin.
Hiz wi wir heids, wir rizzon, wir printit wird;
Them wi their een, their finger-eyns, their midder wit,
Ootlins noo in a warl they widna fit.
Time canna rin back. They'll seen be oot o min'.
We winna see again folk o yon kin'.

---

kennin: *knowing.* rizzon: *reason.* lear: *learning.* traivelt a staig: *walked the roads with a stallion.* styoo: *dust.* skytit: *rebounded.* dreelt: *hustled.* steys: *corsets.* reid-mowsert: *red moustached.* far ben: *well versed.* Horseman's Wird: *Ploughman's Masonry.* suppert: *given his supper.* nyaakit: *naked.* toozy: *tangled.* reengin: *wandering.* geets: *children.* laich-in: *quietly; secretly.* wadgin her nieve: *shaking her fist.* waal: *well.* puddock steels: *toad stools; mushrooms.* oorlich: *miserable creature.* greenichty: *greenish.* skookin ahin: *skulking behind.* breem buss: *broom bush.* fite-winkert: *with fair eyelashes.* drog: *drug.* nott: *required.* nieve-fu: *fistful.* hirplan: *limping.* hyowe: *hoe.* crulgie doon: *shrunk with age.* gey dottelt: *mentally confused.* on the meenit heid: *punctual.* ootlins: *aliens.*

Playin at the Baa

'A common, a whirlie,
One hand, limpie,
Furlin-Jockie, everlastins.'
Faa'll play wi my baa?

Faar'll we play, this Simmer day,
Up the closs or ower the brae,
Or in ahin the rucks o strae,
Faar'll we play wi my baa?

Byre door, barn door,
Henhoose door, stable door,
Faar's a great big muckle door
Faar we'll stot wir baa, baa?

Byre door's aal an deen.
Watch yon nesty slippery steen.
The bailie's in a richt ull teen.
Canna play at baa there.

On henhoose door we manna play.
We'd scare the hennies aff the lay.
The ganner picks. Feart? No, I'm nae!
Canna play at baa there.

Stable door's caal an roch.
Horsies dyste their feet, an och!
Plash goes the baa i the water-troch.
Canna play at baa there.

Bit in ahin the rucks o strae
Far the sin shines aa the day,
Upo the big barn door we'll play,
Here we'll play wi baa, baa.

'A common, a whirlie,
One hand, limpie,
Furlin-Jockie, everlastins.'
Stot-stot goes my baa,
Come an play wi my baa.

rucks o strae: *ricks of straw.* steen: *stone.* ull teen: *bad humour.* manna: *must not.* caal an roch: *cold and rough.* dyste: *stamp, thump.*

The Aal Waal

'Come oot o 'aat, ye puddlin vratch,'
Skraichs the girnie wife at me.
'Ye'll tummle in an droon yersel,
Ye'll catch yer death o caal.
Losh, quine, fit div ye get to watch
In at aal waal?'

Fit div I watch? See yon spoot?
Hear the water trinklin oot?
Kep some in yon roosty mull.
Naebody badders gin ye spull,
Doon b' the aal waal.

I'm feart at yon dark nesty place
Laich ower ere, at the back,
Faar green an slivvery tangles dreep
An emmerteens an gollachs creep,
An poddicks lowp an slaters craal
Roun the eezins o the waal.

Bit I like at place far it's shinin blue,
The colour o the sky;
Far little pansy-faces teet
Atween the steens, an prood an tall
Pink foxgloves boo to see themsels
In their lookin-gless, the waal.

An fyles on a stull hairst efterneen —
Nae braith o win to stir
The smaa fite deukie's fedder curlt
Roun the dry carl-doddie flooer —
I see doon ere the Muckle Furth twaa-faal,
Clood, fleein bird an the toozy heid at's me,
The big warl in a little warl, the waal.

'Come oot o 'aat, ye puddlin vratch,'
Skraichs the girnie wife at me.
'Come awaa fae at aal waal,
Ere's naething ere to see,'
Says she.

waal: *well.* puddlin: *messing about with water.* vratch: *wretch.* skraichs: *screeches.*
girnie: *ill-tempered.* spoot: *spout.* kep: *catch.* roosty mull: *rusty tin.* badders: *bothers.*
laich: *low.* emmerteens: *ants.* gollachs: *beetles.* poddicks: *frogs.* eezins: *eaves.* teet: *peep.*
fyles: *occasionally.* hairst: *harvest.* fite deukie's: *white duck's.* carl-doddie: *ribgrass.*
twaa-faal: *two-fold; mirrored.* toozy: *towzled.*

The Price o Bress

Jess Hedderwick raise at the income o licht
Wi a great clattervengeance o soun.
She wis dystin her basses anent the ga'le dyke
Lang afore Tam the Milkie wan roun.
Wi besom an scrubber she yarkit an breengt.
Fin maist wives were jist teemin their aess.
Her wark wis aa deen, she hid aa the foreneen
To ficher an soss wi her bress.
       Smert Jess!
She hid aa the foreneen tull her bress.

Sax furligorums o cannlesticks
An twaa fancy scallopit trays,
A clock that gid eence an a dishie for preens,
A spunk-box, a bell, a flooer vase,
Pokers an tyangses in hullicks
An toasters hung up on the waa,
A shufflie wi holes at widna haud coals,
An a bellas at widna blaa.

O! Jess wis a notable cleaner,
A champion chaser o styoo.
Ye were feart to set fitt on her waxcloth
Or finger her walnut buroo.
She wis full o her antimacassers,
Her joogies, her tidies, her gless
An made sic a meneer ower her braw chiffoneer,
Bit neen could compare wi her bress.
       Losh, Jess!
Wis clean gyte ower the heids o her bress.

Noo, Jess hid a man they caad Jeemsie
Fa skookit aboot throwe the hoose;
A smaa, snytit oolt-lookin oorlich
Wi as much rumgumption's a moose.
It wis: 'Jeemsie! Ye'll need to hack stickies,'
An: 'Ye'll need to be reddin yon spoot,'

An: 'Gae waa, noo, an sneck in the bantins,'
An: 'Jeemsie! 's the cat putten oot?'

Eence Jeemsie hid been a keen birkie
Fa likit a smoke an a dram,
An antrin bit dirl on 's melodeon,
A nicht wi the rod at the dam.

Bit Jess hooey't him furth wi's melodeon.
'Tak 'Bonnie Strathyre' to the yard,'
Hine doon to the back o the bourtree
Far he'd neither be seen nor be haard.
An Jess haiv't his troots to the midden.
'Their guts-lard, feech, gyaad, sic a mess!'
An she seegt a hale wik aboot Bogie Roll rik,
Foo it blaadit the shine on her bress.
        Quo Jess:
'It clean connachs the shine on my bress.'

So Jeemsie jist tholt an said naething
Till, ae quaet grouthy nicht afore Pess,
He did a meenlichty flittin
Fae the hoose wi the braa, shinin bress.
He gid aff wi the wife fae the chip shop.
She belangt doon the wye o the Broch,
A big strushil deem wi a mowser
An a laach that wis herty an roch.

Twaa neebor wives were colloguin
Ae day they'd been in seein Jess.
'She's gey sair come-at aboot Jeemsie, I doot.'
'Yea? I saw nae odds on her face.'
'Na! Bit did ye nae notice her mantelpiece?
She hisna been keepin her bress.
        Peer Jess!
The shine's fair geen aff o her bress.'

clattervengeance: *uproar.* dystin: *beating.* basses: *door mats.* yarkit an breengt: *slammed things about.* teemin their aess: *emptying their ash.* ficher an soss: *finger and mess about with.* furligorums: *showy ornaments.* tyangses: *tongs.* styoo: *dust.* buroo: *bureau.*

antimacassers: *decorative material protectors for easy chair backs and arms.* meneer: *fuss.* skookit: *skulked.* snytit: *stunted.* oolt-lookin: *cowed.* oorlich: *miserable creature.* reddin yon spoot: *clearing that drain.* bantins: *bantams.* antrin: *occasional.* hooey'd: *chivvied.* hine doon: *far down.* haiv't: *threw out.* seegt: *scolded.* rik: *smoke.* blaadit: *spoiled.* connachs: *dims, destroys.* tholt: *suffered.* grouthy: *good growing.* Pess: *Easter.* strushil deem: *untidy woman.* mowser: *moustache.* colloguin: *gossiping.* gey sair come-at: *very upset.*

Mains o Yawal's Dook

Based on Chapter 5 of *Johnny Gibb of Gushetneuk*
by William Alexander.

The wark's weel tee, the hey's in cole, the mossin's gey near by,
Ben the midden dyke gwana bags hing furth to dry.
The bailie an the orra loon's awaa to Aikey Fair
An Mains o Yawal's aff to tak his annwal at Tarlair.

Oh, blue's the lift abeen the Firth this bonny Simmer day
An blue's the water reeshlin ower the saans on Deveron Bay.
The win blaas saft doon Langmanhull an rare's the caller guff
O tar an raips an dilse alang the sea-wynds o Macduff.

Bit Mains is in a bog o swyte, his winkers fite wi styoo.
He's stecht in's wivven draavers an sair hankit in's surtoo.
He's burssen, fool an yokie an crochlie i the queets.
The verra feet o him's roassen an fair lowpin in his beets.

Wi Mally lowst an stablt noo, he hyters to the shore,
Skytin upo knablick steens an slidderin amo waar.
He's caain for a lippin peel, a lythe an sinny nyook,
For he's dwebble an he's druchtit an he's mangin for his dook.

Briks weel rowet up, his hose an sheen he casts afore his claes
He picks the strabs an yaavins oot atween his crunklt taes.
Syne he tirrs doon tull his middle, hat, surtoo, sark as weel
An, ae fitt syne anidder, he gyangs plype intull the peel.

He raxes for a puckle dilse an scoors his back an front
Wi mony a haach an pyocher, wi mony a pech an grunt.
Syne oot he spangs, his sark an cwyte an hat again he siks
An tirrs up tull his middle, castin wivven draars an briks.

He's lichtsome as a stirkie that's shaaken aff the branks.
A pirl o win plays hey-ma-nannie roun his spinnle shanks,
He splyters in the peel again. Oh, rare an caal an roch's
The gluff o saat sea-water slocknin Mains's gizzent hochs.

Bit dooks, like idder pleesures, come ower seen tull an en.
Ower seen in draars an briks the legs are clossacht up again.
An noo, upo a girssy knowe, he dowps doon, dacent carl,
For this ae oor o aa the year, at peace wi aa the warl.

dook: *dip.* weel tee: *well forward.* gwana: *guano.* orra loon: *odd-job boy.* annwall: *annual; yearly.* lift: *sky.* abeen: *above.* reeshlin: *rustling.* caller guff: *fresh smell.* bog o swyte: *state of perspiration.* winkers: *eyelashes.* fite wi styoo: *white with dust.* stecht: *overheated.* wivven draavers: *men's knitted, long pants.* sair hankit: *constricted.* surtoo: *surtout; old-fashioned jacket.* burssen: *bursting; overheated.* fool an yokie: *dirty and itchy.* crochlie i the queets: *crippled in the ankles.* roassen: *roasted.* lowst: *unyoked.* hyters: *stumbles.* skytin: *slipping.* knablick steens: *knobbly stones.* waar: *seaweed.* lippin peel: *brimming pool.* dwebble: *feeble.* druchtit: *dehydrated.* mangin: *longing.* hose an sheen: *stockings and shoes.* strabs an yaavins: *loose straw and awns (beard of oats).* tirrs: *strips.* raxes: *stretches.* scoors: *scours.* haach an pyocher: *a clearing of the throat followed by a cough.* pech: *gasp.* spangs: *strides.* wivven draars: *woolly underpants.* briks: *trousers.* pirl o win: *gentle breeze.* spinnle shanks: *spindly legs.* splyters: *splatters.* gluff: *shock.* slocknin: *slaking.* gizzent hochs: *dried up legs.* clossacht: *enclosed.* girssy knowe: *grassy hillock.* dowps doon: *sits down.* ae oor: *one hour.*

A Maitter o Status

Jean Haggerty weesh at the Curnel's
An cleant to the minister's wife.
She wis een o the village heid bummers
The better pairt o her life;
A weeda umman, fresh an swack,
Jinniprous an genteel,
A pillar o the Guild an Choir
An the W.R.I. as weel.

Jean hid a loon caad Davie.
He'd a lang ee at Kate Wull,
A tow-heidit, hallirackit deem
Fa vrocht at Gillespie's mull,
Made broth at the mairt an Aikey,
Took days at the hairst an hyowe
An wis aye on the haik for a hyse or a claik
Wi the chiels at the pub in the Howe.

Aabody kent Dave's midder
Hid nae eese avaa for Kate,
So finivver merridge wis mentioned
Jean pat her fitt doon the richt gait.
It wis jist a maitter o status,
The twaa weemen war wardles apairt —
The help at the manse an the Curnel's,
The quine fa skudgt at the mairt.

Nae mair wis hard aboot it
Till a whisper gid the rouns:
('Davie? Nivver! Yon clip Kate?'
'Fa wid hiv thocht it, him sae blate!'
'Hame or daylicht, toozlin's bed?'
'Jean! The price o 'er, bigsy ted!')
Some glowert an preservt themsels,
Idders blusht an blinkit,
Some in boorachs roun the doors
Snichert, swore an winkit.

Deems gyaan eerins to the shop
Nivver wan the linth o't.
Grippie fairmers at the mairt
Steed their haan on the strinth o't.

Bit aa grew eest wi't seen aneuch.
Finivver the dark cam doon
The lad wis ben the mason's lane
An up to the heid o the toon.
Wifies in safties, snibbin back-doors,
Hard him an mummelt: 'Peer sowff!'
An the cadger's bikk wis ower weel acquant
To badder eyven to bowff.

Or the bailie at the dyrie
Hid sneckit aff's alarm.
Or the baker for his mornin baps
Hid mixt the reamin barm;
Lang or the mull-toon cock begood
To hirssle on his reest,
Or the Fite Horse upo Mormond raise
Throwe the sea-haar i the east;

Come sleet or drucht, come smirr or snaa,
Dubs or styoo or slidder,
Dave wis hame an toozlin's bed
An fessin in peats tull his midder.
He wis fyles a thochtie short in the trot
An sanshich in his mainner,
Gantin half wye throwe the foreneen
An needin a flap efter's denner.

First cam a lassockie, neist a loon,
Pows war shakken sair ower Kate.
Bit hans war putten in pooches syne
To help wi hippens an maet.
Some caad them Haggerty, some caad them Wull,
The teen wis as gweed as the tidder,
Though the nackets war scuttert-kin', fyles, at the skweel,
Wi nae fadder, an Kate for a midder.

43

At the linth an the lang Jean slippit awaa.
Watchie Wicht spaak for's aa on the maitter.
'Her? I've kent i ma time a curn far coorser folk
At I've likit a dassint sicht better.'
In twaa-three wiks the spik gid roun —
Claik's aye easy cairriet —
At Dave an Kate, come Mertinmas,
War quaetly gettin mairriet.

Pleased? Fint a fears! Folk humft an glumft
Wi faces maist funereal.
Thraa'd their moos, lat doon their broos.
Merridge? Mair like a beerial!
Yon dressmakker bodsy, fa'd nivver a lad
An wid nivver see fifty again,
She peakit an grat an said, dichtin her een:
'Ech, 'twis shortsome, his fitt i the lane.'

We'd aa a saft side tull yon twaa,
They'd brichtent wir toon sae lang
Wi a fine bittie scandal, a touch o romance.
Faa care't fit wis Richt or fit Vrang?
Fine, noo, at an umman wis gettin her dues
An her femily dacently faddert,
Bit quo wee Watchie Wicht, wi a haach an a spit:
'Tyaach, at their age, fit nott they hiv baddert?'

---

weesh: *washed; did the laundry.* weeda umman: *widow woman.* swack: *agile.* jinniprous
an genteel: *spruce and aping the gentry.* loon: *boy.* lang ee: *long eye; was attracted to.*
tow-heidit: *fair-haired.* hallirackit: *hoydenish.* vrocht: *worked.* hyowe: *hoe.* on the haik:
on the lookout. hyse: *romp; friendly banter.* claik: *gossip.* wardles: *worlds.* skudgt:
drudged. blate: *bashful.* bigsy: *proud; socially conscious.* boorachs: *clusters.* eerins:
errands. grippie: *mean.* aneuch: *enough.* peer sowff: *poor simpleton.* cadger's bikk:
hawker's bitch. weel acquant: *familiar.* badder: *bother.* reamin barm: *foaming yeast.*
begood: *began.* hirssle: *fidget.* reest: *roost.* drucht: *drought.* styoo: *dust.* toozlin:
rumpling. fessin: *fetching.* thochtie: *mite.* sanshich: *curt.* gantin: *yawning.* flap: *snooze.*
neist: *next.* hippens: *diapers.* nackets: *small children.* scuttert-kin: *disadvantaged.*
skweel: *school.* curn: *a few.* fint a fears!: *not likely!* humft an glumft: *dithered.* thraa'd
their moos: *grimaced.* bodsy: *small and dapper.* fit nott they?: *why need they?*

Druchtit

(Lament on the occasion of a dry summer)

Nivver a sign o rain yet, eh?
Fit dis the wireless mannie say?
Stull dry? Anidder bonnie day?
    We're druchtit.

Nivver a troot in Don or Dee,
The only fish are in the sea.
Wir fly-cup's ale, we've nae tay-bree.
    We're affa druchtit.

Nivver a dook for wiks an wiks,
The swyte-draps trinklin doon wir chiks,
Wir hurdies stucken til wir briks,
    We're stecht an druchtit.

Nae mowse this for folk or kye,
Drinkin-trochs gey near bone-dry,
Girss parks birselt broon forbye,
    Clean druchtit.

An awyte it's nae exactly plizzent
To watch yer neeps turn blae an wizzent,
A puckle mildyowt runts, aa gizzent
    An druchtit.

The corn's a mess o yarr an skellach,
The dam's awaa til a dubby hole – ach,
It widna weet the queets o a gollach,
    Sae sair it's druchtit.

The gairden flooers are by wi't noo,
Jist chuckenwort far pansies grew,
An we're holin tatties amon styoo.
    They're druchtit.

The weemen's in a richt ull teen,
Forfochen, canna thole their sheen.
An fit's the eese o a washin-machine,
    Fin ye're druchtit?

It's nae in ony mortal's pooer
To raise the win, bring on a shooer.
Wi Naiter's elements to cope
Is far ootwith oor human scope.
Maybe a bit prayer's the only hope
For folk that's druchtit?

Lord, open noo yer hivvenly foont.
Ower lang on hiz peer breets ye've froont.
Surely we've sattl't wir accoont,
    Sae lang we've smuchtit?
Fit though by spates we're aa maroont,
By howderin heericans dumfoont,
Freestit, drookit, aye, even droont!
    Onything's better than druchtit.

druchtit: *dehydrated.* tay-bree: *tea-liquid.* swyte-draps: *sweat-drops.* hurdies: *hips.*
stecht: *overheated.* nae mowse: *no laughing matter.* birselt: *burned.* awyte: *indeed.*
blae an wizzent: *pale and shrunken.* mildyowt: *mildewed.* gizzent: *dried up.* yarr an
skellach: *corn spurrey and charlock.* queets: *ankles.* gollach: *beetle.* chuckenwort:
chickenwort. richt ull teen: *right bad mood.* forfochen: *exhausted.* thole: *bear; put up
with.* Naiter: *Nature.* smuchtit: *choked up.* howderin: *blustering.* freestit: *frozen.* drookit:
drenched.

Poems
in
English

Flora Garry at the age of ninety-three at Dalginross House retirement home in Comrie, Spring 1994. (Photo: Gordon Wright)

Winter in Angus

Serene on the skyline a great white cat sits,
The curve of his glittering breast on giant paws incurled.
Leonine, malevolent,
He fronts the eastern seaboard
Noonday vigil keeping in a strange heraldic world.

By the black mill stream stirs Archaeopterix,
From age-old slumber struggling to awake,
One webbed wing in air,
Oddly two-dimensional,
Incomplete caricature of bat and bird and snake.

Drab against the snowy field, squatting on his haunches,
Dragon-like, contorted, his fleshy bulk outspread,
Grim Gigantosaurus
Pauses in motion,
Poises his tapering tail and small vicious head.

Herd of hunch-backed tortoises lurches up to high ground,
Deliberately tracking their prey in retreat,
Each mottled carapace
Shrouding in shadow
Downward-peering, evil eyes and blunt vestigial feet.

Harried and fugitive fragments of humanity,
Huddled on the bare slopes, make their last stand.
The white cat sits vigilant,
The dun beasts draw nearer,
I walk afraid and lonely in an alien land.

Only some fir trees, ragged and windblown?
And, down by the lade where the sluice water spills,
A length of broken fencing?
And, by the dyke, potato pits,
And Geordie Martin's haystacks, and the far Fife hills?

Ambulance Depot, 1942

Christmas Eve. The hour between tea and black-out.
The stove reddens and snores in the gathering dusk.
Five tin helmets hang in a row on the wall,
Their little black pot-bellies gleam in the glow of the fire.
Painted on each is a large white capital A.
The telephone stands dumb on its shelf in the nook.
No 'Air Raid Message' comes through, Purple or Red.
The fading sky is void and cold and still
But for the friendly drone of a homing plane,
And the strident intermittent trumpeting
Of the arrowhead formations of the geese
Winging riverwards to seek the sheltering reeds.
In the gloom of the garage the empty vehicles wait,
While we sit here by the snoring stove, and knit.
We are making a Christmas toy, a communal gift,
A scarlet and yellow duck with a bear's snout.

MacDonald is making the head. She had a son.
But his ship, 'overdue must now be presumed lost'.
She carries on as before, brave and bright-eyed.
What can we say? We give her the easiest chair
And fuss with cups of tea and hand cigarettes.
Easier for everyone if she were less brave.

Roberts is making the body of the duck.
She is old. She comes of gentle-folk,
And speaks with an English voice, and avoids draughts.
But she's good at the job and asks for no concessions.
There was someone, we've been told, in the last war.
He fell, leading his men, at Neuve Chapelle.
She likes being here, though we're not quite her sort.
It's something she can do towards settling an old score.

The wings of the duck are made by Clark and Smith
Whose make-up is protective colouration.
They are young. Each wears a wedding ring.
They live from mail to mail, they crouch by the map

And trace the African coast, spelling out names,
Bizerta, Tunis, Tripoli, Tangier,
Renowned in tales of antique chivalry;
Each word a sharp potential two-edged sword
Striking one day, perhaps, at the heart's core.

Watson is making the two feet of the duck.
Leave's postponed. No Christmas engagement now.
They must wait, a few weeks maybe,
Maybe for all time.
She knits, not lifting her head. Best leave her alone.
Shouldn't the black-out be on? We draw the blinds,
Make up the fire – a shovel of dross will do –
Shut out the darkening night and the eerie gusts
Of wind assaulting the hut's ramshackle roof,
Bearing the season's first thin tentative snow.
'Another cigarette? Have you heard this one?'
We laugh, a little too loud. Then silence lasts
A little too long. A muttered emotional curse!
Let's have the wireless on and get the news.
(The news we've learned to hate, but dare not miss.)
A boy's voice sings, high, clear and cruelly sweet:

As we watched at dead of night
Lo! we saw a wondrous light.
Angels singing peace on earth
Telling of the Saviour's birth.

We are making a Christmas toy, a sort of duck,
A comical duck with the blunt, snub snout of a bear.
We are making a toy for some other woman's child.
No one here has any child of her own.

Sutherland Street, W.2.

A far, far cry to Sutherland Street
From moor and loch, seal on the wave-washed rock,
Stag on the hill and eagle in the cloud
And sunset's benediction on the Hebrides.
From Assynt and Benmore, from Eriboll,
Far indeed to the street called Sutherland.

Here the beetling man-made tenement cliffs,
Hewn and chiselled mountain caricatures.
Here the cylindrical peaks of chimney-pots.
Window-gullies, geometric slits,
Like unseeing eyes reject the leaden light.
From close-mouths, as from caves, the people pass
Along the pavement's rigid valley floor.
Shaped like the clothes of the better multiple stores
In the advertisement pages of magazines,
They have pale, withdrawn faces and the look,
Guarded and wary, of the hurt or hunted beast.
They are the comfortable middle class,
Who have never known bodily hunger or stress.
A few will leave to their heirs some small estate.
All have carefully conditioned minds,
Moulded by school and university,
Cinema, lending library, radio.
They think in slogans and in cliché phrases.
They love their class and their respectability.
For an ideology they will fight and die.
Of the line of martyrs, saints and fanatics,
They are civilization's finest flower,
Who daily tread the drab front steps of Sutherland Street.
Now daily they must walk with fear for friend,
With black misgiving seek their beds each night,
The fabric of their dreaming interwoven
With dread of future insecurity.
Such is the northern aspect of the street,
Chill, repellent and impenetrable
Fortress of inviolate gentility.

But look with me from my high window down
On the yards, the back doors and the drying greens.
Look on the southern aspect of the street.
Here stand the dust-bins and the air-raid shelters.
Here are trodden earth and sour grass.
A woman carries a bucket full of ashes.
The garments she wears are work-stained, nondescript.
Clumsy, slow is her dateless female form,
Fashioned by toil and childbirth down the ages.
Moving between the flat-roofed, hut-like shelters,
She is a figure from the dawn of history,
She tilts the dust-bin lid, the grimy zinc
Is harsh beneath her finger-tips, the wind
Swirls the gritty ashes between her teeth.
Here is physical labour, the ebb and flow
Of seasonal cold and heat, of growth and flower;
The new gold of laburnum buds in May
On old and sooty boughs, a dandelion
Shining from a brick wall in July.
Here a young man, whistling, mends a chair,
A young wife hangs her baby-clothes to dry,
Windows are opened, curtains billow out.
Neuter cats sleep curled on sunny sills.
A man in shirt-sleeves washes at a sink.
A woman reads and sips a cup of tea.
A girl at a mirror gravely paints her lips
And music blares from a dozen wireless sets.
This, then, is the back of Sutherland Street.
This is natural man, who loves his home,
His children and his ease; creature of instinct
And of appetite, compelled even now
By natural laws and force of circumstance,
Moulded still by his environment.
But see him stepping down from his front door,
Precisely gloved and hatted, wary-eyed.
Here is Man become Mind, the architect
And builder of his own environment,
Bewildered and appalled by his own creation,
Fearful of his self-appointed destiny.

Perhaps when 'the time of the breaking of nations' is ended,
And life renews itself amid the ruins,
In some far corner, Eriboll maybe,
Or Assynt or Benmore, there will arise
A huddle of stone-built huts. – The night draws on.
A woman, stooping, stirs with a knotty branch
Ashes and sparks from a fire on the bare ground.
A man sits, crouching low, beside the flames.
His look is withdrawn, intent, his whole being
Centred in the motions of his fingers.
With fragments of bone and wood he has made a hook,
A fishing hook, a new and better hook.
The eagle seeks her nest on the jutting crag,
The stag in the grassy hollow makes his bed,
The seal slips seaward on the ebbing tide
And sunset, lingering, gilds the Hebrides.
But man, with his fishing hook, is on the road
That winds through centuries of growth and toil,
Frustration, exultation, agony,
And brings him home at last – we wonder where –
Not, we pray, to a second Sutherland Street.

Bog Cotton

Pick, throw away as you will,
Bluebell and daffodil.
They must pay for your holiday.
Let them unheeded lie
Under heel or wheel,
Or let them die
Untended in the jar upon the window-sill.

Or make a casual posy
Of buttercup and daisy,
Honeysuckle, pansy,
Purple vetch and tansy;
Roadside flowers expendable,
Familiar, plain and cosy.

But lay no vandal finger on that flower-wraith
Bog-cotton, whitening the winds of June
In solitary places where the curlew pipes.
Its chill pointed candle flames
Illumine the high altar of the moor.
Those pale fires swept the primordial wastes
When thaw struck off earth's icy manacles.
They knew the still green twilight of the brooding tundra.
Rooted in raw peat, fed by the alchemy
Of subsidence, compression, sun and rain,
Their feet are set where once the lordly heads
Of oak and pinetree tossed in the salty gales
Blown from the young intrusive sea
Across the ancient forest lands of Caledon.
They knew the circled stone, the priest at his rites,
The hymn to the stars, the blood of the cockerel.

Leave the little torches to the wind's breath.
Keep that white magic far from human door.
No comfort there for man's mortality.
Go empty-handed when you walk the moor.

Decently and in Order

'This our brother.' The mourners with closed faces
Looked at the word and hurled it back at the preacher.
Brother? That old sod, always a chip on his shoulder?
He farmed well, give him his due, none better.
But an arrogant man, hard, miserly, vindictive,
Hag-ridden by curious hatreds and obsessions:
Dogs and poachers, vagrants and trespassers,
Women, the rich, the weak, the unemployable,
White-collar men like lawyers and tax inspectors,
Royalty, politicians, all pretenders to learning,
Dancers and dram-drinkers, poets, makers of music,
Children laughing and playing, growers of roses.

'The love of God that is in Christ Jesus.'
Love of a sort he had known, after his fashion:
Wood and metal and tools, machinery working,
Well-balanced gates that fleetly swung on their hinges,
Smooth-sliding barn doors, tractors, bogies and barrows,
Land and cattle and crops, his long lean byre cats.
But skill he had none of human relationship.

'I am the Resurrection and the Life.'
The mourners sat withdrawn, inscrutable,
Glance nor gesture betraying their minds' turmoil.
He had denied the Hereafter, flesh was but grass,
The rest delusion, bait for fools and hypocrites.
They heard again the defiant querulous bluster
Saw the proud troubled gaze of the ageing atheist
Nailed to the tree of his own intransigence.

The mood of the mourners darkened, turned ugly.
They dug up from their memories' recesses
Ancient grudges, jibes and festering insults.
Obsequies took the colour of reprisal.
In the name of the Father, the Son and the Holy Spirit,
The Day of Judgment and the Ten Commandments,
They chastised with the whiplash of their rectitude

One unlikeable pagan lying weaponless.

They carried him feet first out into the sunlight
(Waste of time, the best hay day all Summer.)
The polished cars and the coach's glasswork glittered.
Into the country town they drove decorously,
Past the garages, villas and railed-in gardens,
To the bright, geometric, well-groomed cemetery.
The wreaths were wilting now. Would they give him a stone?
Granite, of course, with an urn or even an angel.

It should have been far otherwise for him.
Evening and the clover wet with dew.
The time he used to wander by the whin-dykes,
Eyeing fences, cattle-beasts, and water troughs,
Scythe in hand to snick the seeding thistles.
Then would have been the hour of his own choosing,
He in a plain strong box of his own making,
And the farm lads, their spades well-greased and keen-edged,
In a sheltered corner of the sixteen acre.
Just a natural, necessary field job,
Done with competence and expedition,
Prelude to sleep and tomorrow's work and weather.

Fish Queue (1942)

In Friday's queue we meet together,
The one in the felt with the red feather,
The tweedy one in the yellow toque.
(I hate hats) We watch the clock,
Edging along one more pace
Empty shopping-bag, blank queue face.

Behind each unrevealing mask,
Is there – I never dare to ask –
Imaginative compensation
For such suspended animation?
Some formula to alleviate
The tedium of this weekly wait?

I wonder if these dames would know
That children's game of long ago,
'I see something, an it sees me
An I widna gie't for a Scots bawbee.'
Forgotten, if they ever knew!
I'll play alone – the colour's blue.

Delphiniums on an evening in July,
Their stately columns vie
With the evening sky,
Soaring above the orderly disorder
Of the herbaceous border.
(Remember, among all this wish —
Fulfilment, that you're queueing here for fish!)

Cinerarias cloistered under glass,
Sapphire stars in moist still air,
No breath from the outer world can pass
To break the enchantment of their luminous stare.
(The finnan haddocks all away?
Certainly not my lucky day.)

And gentians? Not a few. The mockery
Of two or three stuck casually in the rockery!
But acres challenging the Alpine snow.
They can be temperamental things to grow.

(I hope it chokes her! Snitched, confound her,
My privately pre-selected flounder.)

The game's over. Maybe next week?
A long time in war. You never can tell.
But I know that then my choice will be
Scotland's flower, the little bluebell.
(My turn now in a couple of shakes.
Kippers all gone. Just three fish cakes.)

Says Yellow Toque: 'You don't seem to mind.'
And Red Feather sourly: 'I never find
Any cause for a smile in this ruddy queue.'
Probably daft, but I do.

Rostov-on-Don (1942)

The Mountains of the Caucasus
Invest that foreign sky.
Under the bridge-heads of that Don
Men, dead, go floating by.

Bell heather blooms on Bennachie
Red this bright summer day
And down by Inverurie town
Men work among the hay.

Why should I thole this alien woe,
For dule unkent repine?
The flower of war incarnadines
Another Don than mine.

A Touch of Inspiration

(After a day trip to Aran from Galway in 1963)

I was just looking, I tell you, sitting yonder
And having myself a quiet fag by the stone dyke
Up at the graveyard. And in at the pier
The Galway steamer and visitors trekking
For the postcards, the pub and the jaunting car.
And then I spots them, the three walking women,
Trousers on them and black plastic spectacles.
Folk-lore Commission or such, or college teachers?
Cameras round their necks and them binoculars.
Decent women alright, by the looks of them.
A grey, still day it was and me in no hurry.
I tell them it's glad I am they've brought the weather
And this will be their first time to the island?

After that, you know how it is? They're standing
Gaping about them. 'See yon field?' I asks.
'''Twas Padraig's field. His and his wife Moya's.
Sixty years a-making, the best in Kilmoran.
See there, seven corn stooks, new harvested,
Four good rows of spuds, a patch of clover.'
'Sixty years?' says the woman. (Now I'm away with it.)
'Think you,' I tell them, 'No earth here in the old time
Limestone ridges smooth as ivory
Grey like the hide of an elephant, stony deserts,
Precipices high above the Atlantic.'
Then I'm on to the cruel storms of winter,
The winds raving, the tides trampling,
The red glare of the sunsets.
(Oh, in great good form I was, no boasting.)
And then I speak of the harvest of the sea-weed,
The dark purple sea-weed on the beaches
Cast up by the winds' and waters' fury.
'''Twas then,' says I, 'that Padraig and young Moya
Set themselves to the making of their first field.
Stopping up the crevices with pebble stones,
Shouldering on their backs the sand and sea-weed,
Up from the shore, up the twisty goat-paths,
Spreading layers along the rocky ridges.

Then one warm Spring day, there came to the island,
Over the brown and grey of the barren limestone,
The new grass in its first greening,
The blue-green of the first potatoes' sprouting.'

'Tis a good old yarn, fine for the steamer visitors.
There's the women wiping at their spectacles
And one of them whirring tape-recorders
Catching every word. Thinks I, the pity!
Me in such form, to be wasting their good machines,
The story ended!

'Twas then I had my touch of inspiration.
I spies that old stone cairn by the grave-yard.
There's tears in my eyes and a sob in the throat of me.
Says I to the women, 'There she lies, poor Moya!
God rest her soul. God be good to her.
Not long dead she is, there where we laid her,
Down in her coffin of stones and stones about her.'
'Stones?' say they, whipping out little note-books,
'No earth for the burial? Under cold stones lying?'
'Earth now, is it?' I says, quite quiet and casual like,
'She's well enough. The woman's well enough buried.
Sure, Padraig wouldn't be wasting his little earth field.'
That got them, not a doubt! 'Twas great, the fussing,
Lighting their fags and pointing cameras.

'Moya likes a laugh. Wait till I tell her.
Down at Flanagan's shop she'll be, most likely,
Filling her face with chocolate ice-cream.
And there goes poor Sean Flynn with his jaunting car.
'Twill fall to bits on him, and that horse of his
Blowing and lathered and like to drop in the traces.
Foolish fellow! A touch of inspiration,
And three clean ten bob notes into my pocket.
Decent women they were and civil-spoken.
Shame it would be for visitors off the steamer
To be going without a story from Kilmoran.

To the Glasgow Ballad Club

I saw the untrodden beach, the broken boat,
The croft lands desolate, barn and firehouse bare,
Bracken's creeping pall, the wheeling hungry gull,
Legend there, and memory and unspoken prayer,
But Scotland was not there.

I saw the rich, fat farms along the Carse,
The fabulous herds, the fields of wheat and tare.
I met in the High Street of the county town
The bleak-eyed women's cool, appraising stare.
But Scotland was not there.

I heard the many headed beast on the terracing
Rend with its jungle roar the sooty air,
Unreason's triumph, mass hysteria,
Bagpipe and tartan there and loud-speaker's blare,
But Scotland was not there.

On a darkening afternoon, in a small lighted room,
Above the din of a city thoroughfare,
A few decorous folk, staid and greying folk,
Doucely gathered in friendly session there.

Once the wandering minstrel in story and in rhyme
Interpreted his age and chronicled his time.
What of this assembly here, in our meeting place apart,
Latter-day practitioners of the ballad-maker's art?

Once the minstrel wandered free by tower and dale
Thirled to his harping and the telling of his tale.
But we serve many masters, our distraught minds aware
Of the time's dark, sullen undertones, 'the terror, pit and snare.'

Can we resolve the warring loyalties,
The shams, the doubts, the stresses of the present hour,
Tomorrow bridge with yesterday, view the part and the whole,
Trace out the tortuous growth of root and branch and flower?

Can we distinguish human deed from motive,
Unravel the skein of half-right and half-wrong,
String all the burdensome complexity of living
On the single silver thread of a simple song?

How shall a handful of harassed folk
Fulfil so stern a task?
Rather to put the challenge by, and rest,
Is all we ask.
But we who have savoured the discontent
And joy of the writer's art,
Know that for us there is no release,
Be we never so heavy of heart.

Maybe, in this quiet room
On a darkening afternoon,
From one of our makar band,
At ease reclined in his chair,
Turning the scripted page,
We shall have a new ballad, the voice of our age,
And we shall find Scotland there.

Who Then is my Neighbour? (1964)

A well-remembered pattern, this beginning and this end,
When October brings the students and the scarlet gowns appear.
This paradox of youth and age, new life and withering flower,
The opening of the session and the closing of the year.

The cloisters hold again their echoing footfalls,
The creeping mists their ancient river smell,
The gardener's raking leaves in the college garden
And tingle-tangle-tingle goes the busy college bell.

Then I see among the hurrying crowds the dark-faced men,
And the pleasant autumn idyll fades before my eyes,
No time this for reverie, for smug serenity,
The uneasy question, rather, the solemn, dread surmise.

The age-old deadly challenge that will not brook denial,
New-charged with the sorrows of this grave and troubled hour,
'Who then is my neighbour?' – a strident trumpet blast
To raze the walls of Jericho and fell the ivory tower.

I see the young men crowding to the clanging of the bell,
Pale faces many and dark faces few,
The bell says, 'Hurry, hurry through the gate, don't be late,
Knowledge, college knowledge,
Is waiting here for you.'

*   *   *

In the beginning the god of the sky and the sunlight
Made the great mountains, elephant and lion-shaped.
He made the towering escarpments, the stronghold of
villages and tribesmen down the ages.
There dwelt the blessed spirits of the dead.
But the white man coming with his drills and crowbars
Made a road where no road ever was.
His chariots of fire came puffing white smoke.
Rent were the rocks, the splinters showered the sky.
But the mountain gods were silent, they spoke no word of vengeance,
And the tribesmen watched the road grow longer upon the hills.

From the beginning, over the grassy highlands,
The herdsmen wandered, seeking with their cattle
The grazing ground, the salt-lick and the water-hole.
Their gods were in the vast clouds overhead,
    the winds and the far horizons.
Peaceful in the evening was the herds' homecoming
To the thatched huts, the byres and the cooking pots.
But the cattle multiplied and the rains were tardy,
The grass devoured and the red soil sunbaked,
The red soil cracked and eroded and scoured
By the furious torrents away to the distant flood plains.
The lion and the leopard crouched to seize the straying heifer.
The white man raised enclosures and set them about with thorn fences.

The field-tillers and the furrow-makers
Raised on the foothills their crops of maize and millet,
With hand hoe and digging stick they laboured,
Leading the water trickle over the parched ground.
The women dabbled the seed among the puddles,
Their eyes cast earthwards and their backs bent double.
Their gods were near, among the ochreous rocks,
    the trees, the precious water springs.
But the children multiplied, there was no more virgin soil.
The white man sent surveyors and commissioners,
Cunning were their ways of land price, hard to understand.

From the beginning the impenetrable forest —
There the hunters dwelt, the root-eaters, the honey-gatherers.
To the dark secret glades the outcasts came,
Man owning neither land not beast nor tribe,
Fugitive men, bewitched and hateful to the gods,
Fleeing from their tribal elders' rancour.
But the white man, his Informers and his Forest Guards,
Sought out the deep and hidden lurking places,
Drove out to the clearings the surly forest dwellers.

When the outlawed men, the land-hungry and the famine-fearing,
The uprooted, the aggrieved and the bewildered,
Stealthily met in friendly moonless dark,
They sang together softly,

'The Europeans playing polo,
Ho! We saw them!
The Bwanas and the Mem Sahibs,
Ho! We saw them!
The thin ones and the fat ones
Ho! We saw them!
The chariots of fire, puffing white smoke
Ho! We saw them! When it was dark, with spears and swords,
Down we went!
The night watchman, Ho! We saw him!
But he did not see us. Ho! We slew him!'

Southward then, to the mines and the great cities.
Money, white man's money, waits in the great cities.
Food abundant food, and money in the mines
The streets of Shanty-town are heaped with garbage,
And the shacks of Shanty-town have gaping roofs.
The children play in the filth and stench of the gutters.
The childrens' eyes are festered and their limbs crooked.
But Shanty-town has gramophones and bicycles,
Beads and bracelets, corner-stores and prostitutes.
And money, white man's money, and most of white man's sins.

High in the Matofo hills, on granite boulders resting,
Wind-smitten rain scoured, bleached by the fierce sun,
Austere place of pilgrimage, dedicated tombstone
Of Rhodes who said: 'So much to do, and so little done.'

*   *   *

'Hurry, hurry hurry,' says the bell of the college.
'Come and get it, come and get it,
Knowledge, college knowledge.'
But: 'Who then is my neighbour?' for answer still must wait,
And a voice out of Africa says: 'Late, too late.'

Here the hallowed mingling of spring and old age,
Freedom and tradition, youth and mellowing tree.
But there the swift uprooting, blind violence, black hate,
And from such dire beginning, what shall the ending be?

Two Prose Pieces

Widder an Beasts Maet

We had good neighbours at Auchmunziel. I never heard my mother criticise one of them on account of disobligingness, but sometimes a note of half amused impatience would creep in on quite another score.

'There's Aal Mossie,' she would say, peeping out from the room gable window. 'He'll be needin a news wi your father, I'll awaa an sneck up the deuks, he's affa ae-faul, naething tae spik aboot bit widder an beasts maet.'

Mossie, decent stock, had a one-track mind which dwelt on weather and crops to the exclusion of all else – from what airt the wind, were the clouds lifting away over by Tillyfar, would the frost loup, would the neeps stand another week's drucht?

On the wall by the washstand in our spare bedroom a framed set of verses read:

> Begin the day with God
> Kneel down to him in prayer . . .
> End the day with God.

But our days began with, 'Fit like a mornin?' and ended, 'Fit's the nicht gyaan tae dee?'

God was another dimension altogether, less urgent and apt to be relegated to Sunday and the spare bedroom.

We weren't given at any time to religious observance and if we prayed at all the tenor would have been, 'O Lord thou knowest how busy I must be this day, if I forget you, do not forget me.'

In Buchan we had all sorts of weather and all of it, I recall, larger than life.

The winters were longer and fiercer, summer droughts were severe, the sun shining 'brichter far gin it's ivver deen sin syne,' only a childish illusion?

So I thought, until recently I came across, *The Highlands of Scotland* by O'Neil and Walton and read there, 'If the country is covered by a cold north-easterly air stream bringing Polar maritime air to the region it is the east coast which receives the cold blast. . . . Blizzards and deep snow strike the exposed lowlands of Caithness, Aberdeenshire and Banffshire.'

That old Gulf Stream and its temperate influence never seemed to penetrate as far inland as the hill o Bennygoak.

We had frost, heat, dubs, tearing winds, rainy downpours, the lot.

Although we were only fourteen miles from the coast the sea might have been distant a hundred, were it not for those dense wet ghastly 'haars' that shrouded the summer landscape.

What do I remember of that landscape? The cry of the peesies away over the brown parks in the cold spring gloamings, the summer sky vibrant with larks not seen against the brilliant sun, the drifts of the bog-cotton in the moss, the stooked fields in the autumn, the white wilderness in the winter, then that hill for all seasons, Bennachie, away to the south-west defining the edge of the world, the ultimate point of reference.

'Far ayont Bennachie see the red skies o' gloamin
Hae blawn like the rose and are fadin awa'.'

So says Gavin Grieg in his own lyric.
This was our mountain, part reality, part fantasy.

I once wrote:

'Aye the aal hill stannin there wad seem pairt o baith my wardles,
Lookin doon sae freenly-like at ploo an hairst an hyowe.
Though aften tee the substance o a dream.
The frosty Caucasus anent the Caspian Sea
Soracte far the snaa lay oxter-deep,
Atlas, Athabasca, Helicon, the mountains o the moon were Bennachie.'

But oddly enough it was the countryside at night, the landscape faded out, that made the sharper impact, and that for a very practical reason. Our water closet, or John Gunn, was not at the bottom of the garden. It had its back against the north face of the high stone garden dyke. To reach it you had to open the dwelling-house door, usually in the teeth of a gale, creep round by the porch and the dark best room window and the gig shed door, then you came to the wooden gate in a dyke under a tall elm tree. There was a sneck to fumble with, then you passed through to the wild rough grassy enclosure bordered by bourtrees that lay between the kitchen premises and the sheeps' bucht. A few steps took you to John Gunn's door. But to a small child what a fearsome journey, beset with all imagined and unimaginable hazards!

One wet and gusty night before bedtime, on the verge of tears, I quavered, 'I'm nae gyaan oot, the boodies'll tak me.' 'Nonsense,' said my mother, 'there's nae sic thing, there's naething oot there to be feart at.'

But my father understood. He looked up from his newspaper and said in a casual sort of way, 'Ye needna gyang roon tae John Gunn. Jist toddle ye oot tae the girss aneth the winda an dee yer piddly there.' He knew that it wasn't the things that were there that feart you, it was the things that weren't there – the boodies, the giants, the lepers, the clawing hands. But you didn't want to seem a cooardie so it became a point of honour to make that nightly journey.

Of course there was the 'chantie' below every bed and nobody minded if you used it.

Sometimes you had to, but the challenge of John Gunn had to be met.

In this way I became well acquaint with the dark nights. I could spot the feeble wavering light of a bicycle, the twin lamps of a homeward jogging gig or a lantern crossing Geordie Dalgairn's closs.

Then there were those queer greenish flickerings down in the moss where went the will o' the wisp or the Green Lady. I only half believed that those were just trails of fluorescent water dripping from wings of startled wild duck.

On some nights I went round by the kitchen door and stood by the little dyke there and saw away in the northern sky up where Greenland and the North Pole were, the red, violet and orange veils of the Merry Dancers. When I went inside to the fire and the lamp and asked about them my father would say in to himself.

> 'All night long I watched the streamers
> Flash across the northern sky
> Fearful lights that never beacon
> Save when Kings and Heroes die.'

My mother's comment would be, 'Sir Walter Scott, *Marmion*.'

I didn't like this grown up talk. My Merry Dancers were creatures of grace and light in a fantasied unique world where such mortal considerations as the deaths of kings had no place. A recent popular song has as its theme, 'The Northern Lights of Old Aberdeen'.

Recollections of seasons are so varied, so confused, so dependent on the fallible memory of an old woman for whom the early sharp impact, the 'glory and the freshness' have long since departed.

How much more satisfying to turn to recorded fact, set down at a certain moment in time by one who was at once a practical farmer and a man of wide interests and contemplative habit of mind.

Such a one was James Catto, grandfather of my friend Gavin, who was a little loon at Mains of Culsh when I was a big quine at Mains of Auchmunziel.

The old man left a diary covering the years 1895-1906 from which Gavin kindly allowed me to copy some extracts.

The entries are brief, succinct, vivid, down to earth, touching on most aspects of rural life.'

'Hendry Simpson choked on a bead; fee Maggie Paterson for harvest £4; Ladysmith relieved, great rejoicing; fine sermon by Mr Beveridge on 'The Shield of Faith'; sell old Flo, £12 10/-; Alleson's lecture on Livingstone poor; J. T. commits suicide; pay off lazy Peter 28 shillings, at Bonnykelly sale; kettle 2/6; Chas Souter music teacher visit sung several hymns beautifully; great search for teuchats eggs 2d each; union of Free and U.P. churches.'

Jan. 1895. Wind rose suddenly to almost unequalled hurricane or tornado, tirring houses, over-turning ricks and trees. Great loss by sea and land, sad havoc wrought in woods, we had no ricks over.

Feb. 1895. A bitter weary time, many suffering from want, earth bound in a fetter of iron nothing but picks will remove neeps, country like a stormy sea.

May 1895. Driving showers of hail and blinding dust-fierce drought, things suffering, cold north withering wind, much rain last night, welcome rain, corn sadly stunted.

Oct. 1895. Stoory, full moon, frost-ice.

Oct. 1895. heavy showers of hail and sleet a good deal in store yet.

Feb. 1896. Fine day and fresh, grey soft clouds, soft breeze from west mostly, neeps growing green and laverocks singing.

May 1896. Corn burst – hide a hare or teuchat, grass abundant, tatties briering.

June 1899. Dust flying in clouds-white frost, great heat and drought, ground like flour, many fields resown. Fine gentle rain refreshing all nature, moderate then heavy, oh so welcome.

Oct. 1899. Violent storm, thunder and lightning, hail and rain. Sore trying time for harvest no sooner stuff in a kind of order then on comes the rain – showery every day drizzle.

Oct. 1899. Very fine week could have led the whole crop without a break.

July 1900. Earth soaked with rain, a heartless heavy job, peats a mess.

Aug. 1900. Clyack after many an awkward wearisome travesty about stones and snorled beds of grass and corn, five ricks in.

July 1901. Thunder in the distance coming nearer and nearer, heavy rain and lightning, vivid storm, rages back and fore with alarming violence till midnight, 2 horses killed at Shevado, 3 or 4 cattle at Commonty and a sheep at Hardbedlam and hay burnt at Bulwark.

June 1902. Cold cold! What a bitter equinoctial temp! What bare pasture!

July 1902. Wind north, intense cold, hoe with mittens on.

Aug. 1903. Work nearly at a standstill for rain, rain, the ceaseless rain, the weary rain, from the Kiddshill direction. Pools on lea, stooks drenched to heart.

May 1904. Frost lying white in morning, ice on water, tatties black to earth, many young neeps killed, clover ruinous.

Aug. 1904. Great drought, pasture burned up, weather so pleasant but oh so dry.

March 1906. Wild driven showers of small snow all day, strong frost, piercing cold, the wildest bitterest day for a long time.

Although my mother was somewhat critical of Aal Mossie it was not the content of his conversation she objected to, it was its narrow scope. She was as weather conscious as anybody, but she liked its dramatic colourful aspect. She left no diary from her pen but many articles were published in the *Aberdeen Press and Journal*, one of which I quote. She is recalling the winter of 1879, when snow lay for sixteen weeks, from mid November to mid March.

'I remember the farm kitchen on those stormy mornings, the roaring peat fire and a big water pot on the swey and smaller pots on the binks and brander, the melting snow making a perpetual burn on the flagged floor. When the door was opened, a drift of about eight feet appeared which had to be cut into every morning to let master and men in and out. A big shovel stood in the corner ready for action, for the farm work had to go on, cattle must be fed, cows milked and poultry kept in life. It was a rejuvenating time for mankind and for the land. The belated spring was one of the best on record followed by a glorious summer and a bountiful harvest.'

And so they passed the good seasons and the bad. You had to be tough to acquire a certain kind of fatalism, to have the dogged endurance necessary to put up with the harsh monotony of 'risin-time an lowsin-time and aye yoke, yoke.' When weather and circumstance brought triumph or disaster you had to neither let the one go to your head nor the other knock the feet from you. Old James Catto wanted to be a minister. He became instead a successful, dedicated farmer for whom farming was a completely satisfying way of life. Others took for granted that this was their way of making a living, as it had been their fathers' before them. Some, like my mother, hated it most of the time but gallantly soldiered on, because there was no way out.

widder: *weather.* maet: *food.* news: *chat; to exchange news.* deuks: *ducks.* ae-faul: *one-fold.* decent stock: *likeable chap.* airt: *direction.* loup: *lift; thaw.* fit like?: *what like?; what sort of?* sin syne: *in the past; since then.* haars: *coastal fogs; mists.* peesies: *peewits.* ayont: *beyond.* wardles: *worlds.* hairst: *harvest.* hyowe: *hoe.* anent: *regarding.* sneck: *snib.* boodies: *ghosts.* girss: *grass.* aneth: *beneath.* chantie: *chamber pot.* closs: *close.* Merry Dancers: *Aurora Borealis.* teuchats: *green plovers; lapwings; peewits. Four names for one bird. Teuchats more local to Buchan.* tirring the reefs: *lifting the roofs.* stoory: *wild and windy.* clyack: *corn all cut, but not yet stacked.* snorled: *tangled.* lowsin-time: *time to stop work.* swey: *moveable iron bar over a fire for suspending pots and kettles.* bink: *hob.* brander: *gridiron.* yoke, yoke: *work, work.*

'To See Oorsels'

Address to the Buchan Field Club
New Deer, 14 April 1983

I'm glad to be here, proud but scared stiff. I remember so vividly the respect with which the Buchan Field Club was regarded. As a small girl I heard my parents and elders discussing its deliberations. That in itself tells you something about the people of Buchan. There was a sharp awareness of the things of the mind, but not to the exclusion of loveable human qualities and of earthy everyday affairs. Who has said it better than John C Milne? He saw both sides.

> 'The gweed God-fearin fairmer
> Wi weel-worn wincey sark,
> Wha nivver missed a sermon
> For widder or for wark.'

And then, on the other hand, from 'Fut like folk'.

> 'Thrawn-like folk wha ken but the brods o their Beuk,
> and gang their ain gait wi a lach or a spit or a sweir.'

But don't you worry sometimes about how we in this day and age are presented to the outside world, especially by some writers of modern fiction? So much is distorted, so much is omitted. The emphasis is on the sordid and the nasty, the pre-occupation is with sexual indulgence. Of course sex had its place in the life of a farming community. It was implicit in the air you breathed, in the four-letter words crudely scribbled on the horse stalls, in the begrutten face of the kitchie lass who wouldn't be coming back after the term. And of course publishers demand an emphasis on sex, they have to sell their wares, they're at the mercy of market forces in a so-called permissive age. In the not so distant past there was a much more honest and decent depiction of our Buchan folk-ways by William Alexander, Charles Murray, W P Milne and more recently by John R Allan and Jack Webster. I know this land and its people, the good, the not so good, something of its less worthy aspects. I deplore one-sided, lop-sided presentation. As your editor, Mr White, has so well put it: 'We owe it to unborn generations not to leave frustrating gaps in our culture and history.'

In my own small way I've tried to give an honest picture of our land and people. I'm only sorry that the offering is so meagre. I wish I had my parents' facility. My father wrote for thirty years two, often three, newspaper articles every week. When something 'cam in the wye' my mother stepped in and wrote the articles: she copied his style and nobody spotted the difference, I hope that my little book hasn't let them down.

We lived up the road there in what J B Pratt in his classic *Buchan* calls 'the old mansion house of Auchmunziel'. There were eleven of us, old grandpa, father and mother, two brothers, a kitchie lass and four fee't men, a typical Buchan ferm toon. I was grandpa's bairn and toddled about with him in and around his beloved garden. We both liked big words and he taught me the names of flowers, pelargoniums, antirrhinums and what he called 'Hellicreeshums'. I still remember the taste of his strawberries and white rasps, the scent of the briar rose hedge, the hidey-holes among the myrrh and dockens and, further afield, the old well down by the duck pond. The well was out of bounds and so a fearful fascination. Grandpa lived through the 'Golden Age' of Scottish agriculture, 1850 to 1890 or thereabouts: through his eyes I caught glimpses of a period when, as John R Allan reminds us, 'there was confidence, peace of mind and a large ease in the countryside.' Early impressions are indelible. You can't ignore the past. Hence my discontent with the portrait of Buchan ferm-toon life painted by recent writers. What aspect has been most misrepresented? Just the quality of the folk, their literacy, width of interests and kindly family affection. In monstrous contrast think of Lewis Grassic Gibbon's two farmers, Blaweary and Meiklebogs. The one is dehumanised by hard toil, bewildered by emotional and sexual conflicts, the other a horror, avaricious, cruel, lecherous behind the sly sleekit smile.

Let me tell you about a real farmer, William Chalmers. He farmed Mains of Oldwhat-Aalfat, a few miles from New Deer, and was my great-uncle by marriage. With emigration in mind, he went out to Oregon to look for land. Here is how he wrote home to his wife:

Diggle's Hotel, Liverpool
1st June, 1870.

Dearest on Earth,

I take this opportunity of writing you as it may be my last at this time this side of the Atlantic. I did not say to you that I go steerage; but I have been strongly induced to do so on account of the company I have got. Several young men of whom I know nothing are among us, two of whom, I have no doubt, are experienced Christians and will readily take their turn in conducting worship which we have regularly here and expect to have aboard ship. Don't be over-anxious about me, for you know that wherever I go I have a Father in the promised land, and may He be graciously with you in my absence is the sincere prayer of

Your ever-loving William.

P.S. There is a great bustle just now, the cart's coming to take down our stuff – every one being provided with bed and blanket and there is a bunch of white-iron or two, like what they carry down to you from the Redhill.

with thousands to you (kisses)
and little Peggy and Mary
W.C.

He bought land, uprooted himself and his large family and started all over again in Oregon. So successful was he that he and his wife were able to come back on a long visit to friends and relations in the Old Country.

The following poem was written by my grandfather James Metcalfe to welcome them home.

Auchmunziel, Aug. 5th, 1884.

Dear Brother and Sister, how delightful to greet thee
In Scotland, auld Scotland, how pleasant to meet thee,
To look in your faces, to hear your voices,
To be clasped once again to your heart's fond embraces.
We've been severed from thee, over ten years and three.
How often we've thought that we ne'er might you see.
We have dreamed of your home and with you gone along
And your fruit trees and woodlands have wandered among.
But now in the land of burn and the heather
The land where the lark and the nightingale sing
We meet you and greet you and ramble together
'Mong the old sights and sounds that sweet memories bring.
The song of the blackbird and mavis sounds clearer
The broom and the heather seem brighter in hue,
And the old friends we meet, somehow they seem dearer
That now we enjoy all these pleasures with you.

Thanks, thanks for your coming, may it aye give you pleasure,
When you think of the friends, oh so friendly to you.
And when you go back to your heart's dearest treasure
Your own ones, your fond ones, so loving and true,
May you still look back gladly on old Scotia's shore,
For the friends hold you dear you'll have left far away,
And we'll aa meet again and be severed no more
In that holy, that sanctified everlasting day.

James Metcalfe, Aged 52.

I grant you Victorian sentimentality and uninhibited expression of religious faith. But these forebears of mine were writing in a strange language, English, broad Scots was their normal speech, they had little schooling. My grandfather went to a dame's school at Cairnorrie, carrying a peat (for the school fire). The wonder is that they could produce this sort of thing at all. If the language was artificial, made familiar mainly through the Bible and newspapers, the sentiments weren't. These were decent, kindly human beings who had standards and tried to live up to them, who had lively, inquisitive minds, concerned not only with 'widder an beasts maet'. I remember one Sunday afternoon, after the kirk had skailed, two village shopkeepers were at the door having a news, we'd had a visiting preacher that day, not our own Mr Beveridge, I was a schoolgirl at the time. Said one to the other: 'Aye, min! Nae a bad sermon.' 'Weel, I dinna ken,' said the other, 'Ye could maybe caa't a learned kin o a lecture, bit it wisna my idea o a sermon.' Lecture? Sermon? What was the difference? Something for a young quine to puzzle over on the road home to her broth and boiled beef. Here was the objective, analytical approach, not always comfortable to live with, but always stimulating. And once, at home, a few neighbours were in for the evening. One of the wives cam ben to the kitchen to look for my mother who asked: 'Is the folk in there aye newsin?' 'Oh, aye, they're giein Free Trade an Protection a tak throu han.' 'Awa, than, an tell them to come ben for a bit supper, afore they get yokit in tull Free Will and Predestination, or they'll be here aa nicht.'

We liked to know the prevailing climate of opinion, what the minister and the local M.P. were thinking. We hadn't many books, but we devoured the daily and weekly papers. They gave Buchan a window on the world. George Bruce, the poet, once remarked: 'You know, when I was a loon in Fraserburgh, we folk in the herring trade had close contacts with the Continent and with all the Baltic ports. There was an exchange of culture.' The postie carried letters from the ends of the earth to our villages and ferm toons. There would be a leopard skin rug in front of a parlour fire, ebony elephants on a mantelshelf, in a lobby window, a cage of tiny blue and scarlet stuffed birds from Brazil. We weren't just a remote, ingrown, rural community. This is an aspect of our life which has been overlooked.

Another aspect that has not been completely explored is the love-hate relationship between land and those who serve it. Sometimes, when we found the daily darg unendurable, when we tire't o plyterin oot an in, were sick of dubs and sharn, then our thoughts turned to far away places. I had this in mind when I wrote 'Foo Aal's Bennachie?'
Lewis Grassic Gibbon knew all about it. He himself had opted out, choosing another kind of servitude, that of books and thoughts. But he made Chris Guthrie stick to the land, tholing all it, and the people on it, could do to her. My crofter lass in 'Bennygoak' did the same for the sake of her old mother.

'Bit ma midder's growein aal an deen
An likes her ain fireside.
'Twid brak her hert to leave the hull:
It's brakkin mine to bide.'

The way of life in the croft and cottar house has been very adequately portrayed in recent writing. David Kerr Cameron's *Willie Gavin, Crofter Man* is an objective, well-documented study which brings alive much that was almost forgotten. And of course Jessie Kesson and David Toulmin, out of their own experience, have dealt with the same subject. I admire the power, vividness and compassion of their writing although the sexual theme is over-emphasised.

The little world of the middle-sized ferm toon, that self-contained interdependent complex of farmer, wife, children, kitchie lass and chaumer men has never been explored in depth. What a wealth of material is there, in the clash of personalities, emotional relationships, social strictures and taboos, the incessant demands of work and animals, the physical pain of muscles stressed to the limit of endurance.

But it was not all back-breaking toil. My father used to recall his first dancing lesson as a young loon. It was held in the barn. A wisp of hay was tied round one ankle, a wisp of straw round the other. The fiddle struck up and away they went: 'Hey fitt, strae fitt, te-daddydum, te-daddydum.' And when dancing days were over there were other kinds of recreation. I'd been re-reading *Johnnie Gibb of Gushetneuk* and chuckling over Mains o Yawal's outing to the waals at Tarlair. I was right back to past days of serenity, contentment and simple pleasures.

What about the women folk and their pleasures and recreations? If we are to believe modern fiction the picture is not pretty. The W.R.I.'s? That's wifies clutching jars of marmalade, out for a bit of scandal-mongering. The Agricultural Show? That's where farmers fake their nowt beasts to cheat the judges. After the wedding, the minister has been discovered in the hay with a deem!

Even for John R Allan the whole scene has little light or colour. This is how he saw it. 'If you stand above Cairnorrie, which is the gate to central Buchan, you see field after field and to every six or eight fields a grim grey house with one tree at the gable end. It is a utility landscape of the very barest kind with no refreshment for the eye or spirit.' For me however there is dignity in the rolling expanse of well-tilled fields and beauty in the great sweep of sky from horizon to horizon. And was it not this same utility landscape that drove us to search out our own inner resources of mind and imagination, to create beauty in sound, in colour and in design? To me as a child and young girl, music was part of living – Victorian ballads and Scots songs in the 'best room' where the piano was, music hall ditties from the deem in the kitchen, bothy ballads in the chaumer.

I thought, coming in at that door tonight, if this hall could speak, what a story it could tell. (New Deer Public Hall.) Here was the centre of our social and cultural life which has never been properly recorded and evaluated. Our love for bonny things had an outlet here, in our Flower Shows, Sales of Work, Dramatic Performances. I think of Gavin Greig's 'Mains's Wooin'. It was the first play I ever saw, I was a little girl of ten, I still remember where I was sitting. I think of the concerts, the singing, the fiddle playing. Once taking part in a concert was that 'shy genius of the Strathspey', our own Jim Dickie; he was playing the 'Cradle Song'. On a front seat was a village worthy, aal Peter Still, gazing up entranced, completely carried away, tears streaming down his cheeks. 'Fut like folk?' Don't you agree that we haven't been well treated by recent writers, that a flawed image is being held up to posterity? Can the Buchan Field Club come to the rescue? Follow in the footsteps of Pratt? Do as Hamish Henderson did with John Strachan, get old people talking, put them on record before memories fade? For we are a distinctive racial group, retaining virtues and perhaps some few vices once typical of the folk of our whole North-east lowlands. Let George Bruce have the last word.

'This is the east coast with winter
Written into its constitution,
Its men know their shortening day
Drops quick into night.
They have developed that
Deliberate and acquiring mind
That comprehends facts
And acts.
Their fat lambs dance on green pastures.
Let us praise them.
They have made the land good.
Praise them.'

gweed: *good*. wincey sark: *shirt made of wincey cloth, a mixture of wool and cotton*. widder: *weather*. thrawn-like: *resistive; obstinate*. brods: *covers; boards (of books)*. gang their ain gate: *go their own way*. lach: *laugh*. begrutten: *tear-stained*. kitchie lass: *kitchen maid*. fee't men: *hired farm servants*. ferm toon: *farm house and steading*. white-iron: *tin-plate*. skailed: *emptied*. tak throu han: *discuss*. yokit in tull: *started in on*. darg: *routine*. plyterin: *messing about in the wet*. sharn: *cattle excrement*. chaumer: *a sleeping chamber for farm workers*. chaumer men: *farm labourers housed in a chamber, part of or near the steading*. nowt beasts: *cattle*. fut like folk?: *what sort of people?*

78

The back road, Mains of Auchmunziel, New Deer, 1953. (photo: unknown)

The original farm house at Auchmunziel was built in 1710 but a back wing was added in 1890 of which the upstairs windows are shown. The dower house of the small estate of Manar, Cairnbanno and Auchmunziel, it was owned by the Gordon family. Later, these were combined in the large estate of Brucklay owned by the Dingwall-Fordyces. Until 1918, the farmers were tenants, paying rents to the lairds, but then my father bought Auchmunziel and since 1957 it has been owned by the Dalgarnos, who were neighbours.

The word Auchmunziel is Gaelic meaning 'a field near the moss'. We had a moss and a peatstack. There were eleven apartments, including the original wine-cellar in the basement where we stored potatoes and called it 'the tattie hole'. We had to feed eleven people three times a day. Wine was never on the menu. The house is separated from the steading by a little but-and-ben, which was the men servants' sleeping quarters. The old mansion house had come down in the world!

The back road leads to a main road and the village of New Deer. We went to school that way. The view from the top is one of the best in Buchan stretching over farm land for thirty miles to the Back o Bennachie. The front road leads down to the main road to Fyvie and Inverurie and back to New Deer.

Auchmunziel was always one of the most desirable farms in the district. I sometimes sat with Grandpa on a seat in the garden and he would say, 'Aye! it's a bonny hame'.